Managing Yourself

In Charge
Series Editor: Roger Cartwright

Managing Yourself

A COMPETENCE APPROACH TO SUPERVISORY MANAGEMENT

Roger Cartwright • Michael Collins
George Green • Anita Candy

Copyright © Roger Cartwright, Michael Collins, George Green and
Anita Candy 1996, 1998

First published 1996
Revised and updated edition printed 1998

Blackwell Publishers Ltd
108 Cowley Road, Oxford OX4 1JF, UK

Blackwell Publishers Inc.
350 Main Street, Malden, Massachusetts 02148, USA

British Library Cataloguing in Publication Data

A CIP catalogue record for this book is available from the
British Library.

Library of Congress Cataloging in Publication Data has been applied for

ISBN 0-631-20925-5 (Pbk)

Typeset in 11.5 and 14pt Palatino
by Photoprint, Torquay, Devon and Getset, Eynsham, Oxford
Printed and bound in Great Britain
by Athenæum Press Ltd, Gateshead, Tyne & Wear

This book is printed on acid-free paper

Contents

What the In Charge *series is all about – intended use; the culture you work in; functional, personal and organizational competence; The MCI Standards – the Personal Competence Model; how the volume is laid out.*

The scenario for the case study supporting In Charge, Managing Yourself.

Do I want to stay here? Why do I want to change my situation/viewpoint/competence? Why am I going on this journey? BACK (Baggage, Aspirations, Culture and Knowledge), PEST (Political, Economic, Social and Technological), SWOT (Strengths, Weaknesses, Opportunities and Threats) analyses.

What do I know about my destination? What are my personal plans? Managing change; positive thinking; planning; excellence.

Relating to others; sensitivity; conflict; resource management; obtaining commitment; personal learning and development; managing stress.

List of Figures

For June, Yvonne, Bronwen and Philip

We would like to express our grateful thanks to all those who have provided help and criticism during the preparation of this volume of *In Charge*.

Liz couldn't believe it. She'd always considered Simon, the area manager, to be too grand to bother about the people like her; and yet during the interview for the deputy branch manager position, he'd shown that he knew a great deal about her work, not just what she'd done but how she'd done it.

Now he'd telephoned her and offered her the post of deputy branch manager at one of the suburban branches of the travel agency she'd worked for for the past four years. It would mean a welcome move out of the city centre into the suburbs – less travelling and fewer problems with the traffic. The money would be useful too; the small building firm her husband Alan had inherited was suffering at the moment.

She had been worried at her lack of managerial experience – although she had a BTEC (Business and Technology Education Council) Certificate in Travel and Tourism – but Simon had offered her a place on the company's 'Management Development Programme'; 'It's at NVQ4' he'd told her. She'd have to find out what an NVQ was later. He'd also told her that she would be in direct charge of many of the day-to-day operations at the branch, freeing the manager, John, to concentrate on the development of business travel.

'Come to think of it', she thought as she put the telephone receiver down, 'why isn't John telling me?' She was doubly surprised as she'd thought that John had been very cool at the interview and she'd come away convinced that she hadn't done very well.

'Well I expect I'll find out how he feels soon enough,' she thought, and began to list her immediate thoughts:

The money would be useful . . .
What about the responsibility?
What would the staff think?
How much extra time would it take?

She'd accepted the job, but as she went to tell her husband one question above all others kept coming back into her mind:

'He's told me I'm going to be IN CHARGE . . . but what does that actually mean?'

Introduction

WHAT IS MANAGING YOURSELF ABOUT?

This book is about personal competence and hence personal success for the supervisor or manager, or indeed the aspiring supervisor and manager.

In recent years there have been a number of books on personal drive, positive thinking, achieving success, etc. that have promised to change your life if you read them from cover to cover. No book can achieve success, only you can do this. There is no magic formula, but there are techniques and ways of thinking that can make your job as a supervisor or manager not only less stressful but will allow you to achieve more of your personal goals – this is what this volume of the *In Charge* series sets out to do. It is designed for all those who want to 'do things better' and gain more enjoyment from their job and life.

Success at work, home or in the community is not just a matter of what you do, but how you do it. This book looks at the personal skills and competences required to make a success of the ventures you are involved in. By considering the actions of people, the book considers the personal factors relating to success and ways of improving and achieving desired outcomes.

WHAT IS THE *IN CHARGE* SERIES ABOUT?

The first three volumes in this series, *Managing People, Managing Activities* and *Managing Resources and Information* are designed to provide those in supervisory and first-line management positions with the knowledge and skills to carry out their supervisory and management tasks with competence. This fourth volume, *Managing Yourself*, is designed for all those in a management or supervisory position who wish to improve their personal competence.

WHO THE SERIES IS INTENDED FOR

If you have responsibilities for others within your organization or you are seeking such responsibility, you will find this series useful. You may have been in your post for some time, you may recently have been promoted or you may be seeking promotion: in all these cases, this series will provide you with useful knowledge and understanding to support you within the work situation, and will aid you with your managerial/supervisory and personal development.

The series is equally relevant to all areas of work and contains cases from the private, public and voluntary sectors.

The series also provides useful material for those responsible for training at this level and has been specially designed to support National Vocational Qualification (NVQ) or Scottish Vocational Qualification (SVQ) programmes at Level 3 Supervisory Management. This fourth volume, *Managing Yourself*, is less specific about level and will be useful to all those in supervisory and management positions as well as individuals undertaking any level of management development programme, especially those at NVQ and SVQ levels 3 and 4.

PROGRAMMES FOR WHICH THE VOLUMES WILL BE USEFUL

Managing People, Managing Activities and *Managing Resources and Information*, the first three volumes of *In Charge*, were written to support supervisory and first-line management development programmes at NVQ or SVQ level 3, in addition to company short courses and individual development. Experience in use has shown that the volumes have also found favour in higher level programmes where the content has served as a useful 'aide mémoire' for students.

Should you decide to undertake formal supervisory or first-line management development, the whole *In Charge* series will be of considerable benefit, written as the volumes are by a team whose experience includes practical management in both the private and public sector, and many years working on and producing management development programmes for supervisors and managers. This volume will be especially useful to those who do not wish for a formal qualification but seek to improve the way they operate.

HOW TO USE *IN CHARGE OF YOURSELF*

No set of books, however well written, can provide the answer to a specific problem that an individual has encountered. However, by providing the individual with an insight into the processes that are at work within situations and with opportunities to examine situations from a variety of standpoints, books such as those in the *In Charge* series can allow the supervisor and manager to make more informed decisions.

How an individual uses this book will depend on the situation they find themselves in. It might be that:

1   you are taking a one-year supervisory or management course and have been advised to read chapters 6 and 7 to support your classroom work. In that case you should consider the material in the light of the lectures and seminars you have attended and use the information in the book to support the taught input;

2   you may be involved in an open-learning programme, in which case the books can add to the information contained in your programme;

3   if you are attending a company-based short course, the book will provide you with extra information and can be used to explore areas that you have developed a special interest in;

4 perhaps you have been newly appointed into a supervisory or management position. *In Charge*, first read systematically and then used as an aid for specific problem areas, will provide you with the knowledge and understanding necessary to perform your new responsibilities;

5 if you have been in a supervisory or first-line management position for some time and you wish to gain further knowledge, or you are seeking further promotion, *In Charge* will provide you with the language and concepts necessary to develop.

This volume, *Managing Yourself*, is different to the other three in the series. They deal with specific functions of supervision and management, while this book deals with the way in which an individual supervisor or manager supports his or her 'functional' role through their personal competence.

Use this book as you would a handbook: scan through first to gain the flavour of the subject, and then you can home in on specifics.

THE CULTURE YOU WORK IN

Fons Trompenaars, in his book *Riding the Waves of Culture*, describes culture as:

The way in which a group of people solves problems.

Another way of looking at this is that culture is a function of the VALUES, ATTITUDES and BELIEFS of a group, be it a national group or a work group. This can be simply stated as 'the way we do things around here'.

We are all aware of the cultural differences between Western and Eastern ways of thinking, perhaps even of the different cultural norms within the EEC; we know from countless television series that despite a common language and many common roots there are considerable differences between the way things are done (the values, attitudes and beliefs) in Britain as against in the United States.

The organization you work for has its own culture (and possibly a series of subcultures); indeed it is the culture that provides the uniqueness to an organization. The authors of this book have spent a great deal of time working with Shell and British Airways – both successful companies and yet both very different in the way they do things. Shell (or Royal Dutch Shell to give the company its proper title) traces its roots back to the Netherlands; British Airways to British European Airways (BEA) and the British Overseas Airways Corporation (BOAC) – very different backgrounds, hence very different cultures. British Airways is an interesting case because it has undergone a recent culture change from a bureaucratic public (nationalized) company to a thrusting, entrepreneurial private-sector concern.

Organizational culture is also a key factor in the case studies at the end of this book, in chapter 9. Taken from life, with the permission of the organizations concerned, the study looks at the links between culture and personal competence, and how these combine to provide an excellent product/service for the customer.

Whatever you do needs to be considered within the context of your work culture, your home culture and your national culture. Supervisors and managers live in a three-dimensional world:

The supervisor/manager at work
The supervisor/manager at home
The supervisor/manager as a member of society

This can be illustrated diagrammatically as in figure 1 (below).

The three circles in figure 1 overlap, but in some cultures they overlap more than in others. In Japan, work, society and home are very much interrelated. In the UK we often separate out home and work.

Whatever success you are aiming for has to be seen within the context of your three overlapping cultures. Culture provides a framework for behaviour and may act as either a limit to success or a spur to it. In many Japanese companies your entry level into the firm decides how far you can rise; this is less likely to be true in a US organization. We will consider these concepts later in this book.

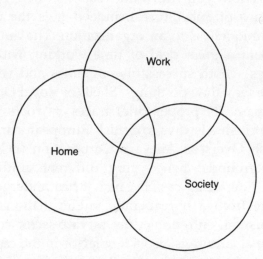

Figure 1 The three dimensions of life

WHAT IS COMPETENCE?

The Concise Oxford Dictionary (2) defines competent as:

  a) adequately qualified or capable
  b) effective

How does one judge effectiveness or capability? The traditional approach to management or supervisory development was based upon standardized inputs; a set course of study, knowledge workshops, etc., followed by some form of away-from-work examination. This form of development was able to test how much the participant had understood the concepts, but it was unable to test for them in actual work situations.

A competence approach uses evidence gained either from the workplace or from work-related simulations to measure the effectiveness not of the learning but of the actual participant. To accomplish this requires a set of national standards against which competence can be measured.

A good example of a competence approach is the driving test. The examiner judges each person against a set of national criteria. How a person learnt to drive is unimportant, the test measures whether they are a competent driver on the day.

However, to drive competently requires more than just undertaking a short test, it also requires knowledge and understanding, hence the Highway Code test. People taking their test do not normally do so using the exact right turns, parking exercises, etc., that they practised on, so they need the understanding necessary to transfer from the practice exercises to those on the test.

The ability to be a safe driver also depends on the personal attributes that you bring to the task. Demonstrating a knowledge and ability to control a vehicle is not enough; safety is part of a state of mind, a way of thinking, a mind-set (to use a phrase you will meet later in this book) – this is the personal competence that needs to be brought to the task.

THE MANAGEMENT STANDARDS

Just as the driving test is measured against national standards, so the competence of a supervisor or manager can be similarly measured.

The Management Charter Initiative (MCI) is the lead body for developing management standards in the United Kingdom. At the time of writing (1997) standards have been developed at four levels:

Level 6		Senior Managers
Level 5	N/SVQ5	Middle Managers
Level 4	N/SVQ4	Junior Managers
Level 3	N/SVQ3	Supervisors

The standards allow a person to judge their competence in an objective manner by seeing how the way they perform tasks matches up to the national criteria.

Because the standards are based more on what a person does than on what they know, they are of equal use to those undertaking a course of study and those who only wish to know more about their own effectiveness.

The standards, as revised in 1997, are arranged in 7 key role areas

| Manage Activities | Manage Resources |
| Manage People | Manage Information |

these areas are covered by the *In Charge* series but there are also standards that relate to:

Managing Energy, Managing Quality and Managing Projects for those in specialized managerial roles.

DEMONSTRATING COMPETENCE

How do you demonstrate competence? In the main you can only demonstrate that you are competent at a task by carrying out that task to a defined standard.

There are only two states attached to competence:

COMPETENT	• having provided sufficient evidence of competency
NOT YET COMPETENT	• having provided insufficient evidence of competence

Those in the latter category are working towards competence.

Liz, who you met at the beginning of this book, could use the Management Standards to put 'meat on the bones' of her job description. Her job description would tell her what tasks she has to perform, the Management Standards would advise her as to how she could judge her competence at those tasks. The *In Charge* series provide the underpinning knowledge and understanding she will need. She would use the Personal Competence Model to assist her in assessing how well she was performing and matching her work experiences against her personal goal.

An important feature of the Management Standards is their applicability across jobs. The same standards apply in public, private and voluntary sector firms and organizations. The tasks and context of the tasks change but the managerial competences remain as a constant.

To demonstrate competence, Liz needs to examine the relevant sections of the Standards and see if she could provide evidence, if required, to demonstrate her competence. If Liz decides to acquire a supervisory qualification by a competence route she will be asked to provide a portfolio containing such evidence from her workplace.

Competence-based programmes are assessed not by the use of the traditional written essay, but by the production of a 'portfolio of evidence', containing such items as work documents, personal reports, and witness reports written by superiors, colleagues, subordinates and even customers. Should you embark on a formal competence programme, you should receive full details of how to build up your portfolio.

In considering her competence and the evidence she would use, Liz needs to think about how relevant and current the evidence is, and how it matches up to the standards.

PERSONAL COMPETENCES

The functional competence areas – **people, resources, activities** and **information** relate to the functions the supervisor or manager carries out. They can be considered as **functional competences**, i.e. as directly related to the job the supervisor or manager does. There are also a set of competences that relate to the personal attributes needed to be a competent manager at any level, from supervisor to senior manager. These are known as **personal competences**, and form the subject of this book.

The functional volumes of the *In Charge* series cover the functional competences in some detail, although there is a consideration of the personal competences at the end of each volume. *In Charge of Yourself* centres on the personal competences and thus complements the other three volumes, although like them, it is designed to stand alone.

Following the MCI guidelines the Personal Competence dimensions are grouped or 'clustered' as follows below in Figure 2, each cluster having a set of 'associated behaviours' that relate to it (the full model including the associated behaviours is included in the appendix at the end of this book).

We owe the authors and generators of the Personal Competence Model a great debt. They have produced a set of personal competences that you can take and adapt to your situation. The scenario that follows in this book is designed to show you how personal competences are used and developed within a work situation, and the benefits that accrue to both the individuals and the organization.

Throughout the Personal Competence Model in the appendix you will note words like, 'develop', 'actively', 'continually', 'commitment', etc. These are words which are associated with personal growth. This book is about growth – your growth as a manager or supervisor and the growth of those for whom you have responsibility.

Personal competences are harder to assess but should not be ignored. Much of the initial work on management competence was carried out by John Burgoyne and his co-workers, and they

---

MCI suggest that for supervisors and managers to perform effectively they should consider the following personal competences.

Acting assertively

Behaving ethically

Building teams

Communicating

Focusing on results

Influencing others

Managing self

Searching for information

Thinking and decision taking

Figure 2 The MCI Personal Competence Model

developed a set of 11 areas of competence that they considered to be very important for those in supervisory or management positions. These are:

1 *Command of the basic facts*:
   to ensure that supervisor/first-line manager is well in-formed about organizational developments, customer needs, relevant data, etc.

2 *Relevant professional knowledge*:
   the supervisor/first-line manager needs to be aware about professional developments within the field of supervision and management and the potential implications of social, economic, legislative and environmental changes on their organization and their role within that and other organizations.

3 *Continuing sensitivity to events*:
   the skills necessary to become attuned to organizational situations and the analysis of situations from a variety of standpoints, and the capacity for further responsibility and the sensitivity to changing situations and demands.

4 *Problem-solving, analytical and decision-making skills*:
   understand the steps involved in effective decision-making, collecting and using data, and monitoring processes and evaluating outcomes.

5 *Social skills and abilities*:
   to improve communication in the work situation, provide strategies for the resolution of conflict, and provide insight into team functioning.

6 *Emotional resilience*:
   to gain in self-confidence and provide strategies for dealing with stress and time management.

7 *Proactivity*:
   to improve flexibility and responsiveness to changing situations and demands.

8 *Creativity*:
   to enhance the capability to seek effective solutions to supervisory and managerial problems.

9 *Mental agility*:
to develop the ability to grasp things quickly, to switch from one problem to another.

10 *Balanced learning habits and styles*:
to develop a range of learning strategies that the participant can use to assist in the work situation; and to manage personal current and future developments.

11 *Self-knowledge*:
to be aware of personal strengths, weaknesses, opportunities and threats so as to retain a high degree of self-control over personal actions.

THINK POINT

Consider the 11 'Competences' quoted above. Think of questions that you can ask yourself to see if you have development need in that area, then place your development needs in priority.

The team that wrote this book have considered a third set of competences, ORGANIZATIONAL COMPETENCIES, or those competences that the organization as a whole needs to possess for success, ability to react to change, seeking new markets, and so forth. Concepts such as BS 5750 and Investors in People may be seen to form part of the make-up of organizational competences.

The role of competence in linking the overall goals of an organization with the tasks performed within the organization can be shown as in figure 3.

One of the first questions often asked when somebody obtains their first supervisory or management job, a question that was uppermost in Liz's mind, is 'What will I actually be doing?'

Supervision and management means taking charge; taking charge of people, operations and/or resources. Supervision and management can be described as 'getting things done through the activities of others'. Often it will mean having direct responsibility for others, but in some cases one will merely be reliant on others, having no direct control over their activities but needing

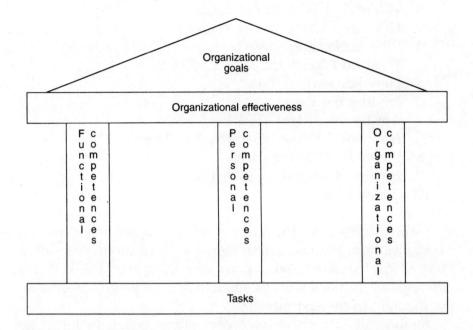

Figure 3 Organizational effectiveness – a competence model

their co-operation in order to ensure that your tasks are carried out.

The Personal Competences are examined, in this book, as a journey. Journeys may occur on a physical dimension (as in London to Manchester), or in a time dimension (my job last year and my job this year), or in a mental dimension (how I acted and thought then as opposed to the way I act and think now). These dimensions overlap, but one dimension often predominates. In the case of the supervisor or manager's personal competence there will be a blend of dimensions.

The chapter headings reflect the 'journey to success', commencing with a scenario that runs throughout the book and serves to set ideas and concepts relating to personal competence in a work context. Chapter 2 introduces you to the characters and organization, and thereafter you will see how they manage on their 'journey to success'.

1 The Scenario
2 Where am I Now?

Throughout or at the end of each chapter there will be examples from the scenario designed to illustrate the consideration of the concepts and actions demonstrated. 'Think Points' throughout the book will ask you to reflect on your own situation in the light of the text material.

At the end of each chapter you will be asked to fill in the relevant section of your personal 'Action Plan' to be found at the end of the book; this is a key activity that will help you monitor your 'journey to success'. Examples of action plans based on the scenario characters will be found at the end of each chapter.

1
The Scenario

You have already briefly met Liz at the front of this book. Liz, her colleagues and their customers, plus their families, form the scenario around which this book explores the concepts of personal competence. Whilst the situations they encounter are, by definition, unique, they are based on real-life examples and you should be able to relate them to your situation and experiences. Indeed, if you consider the personal competences and their associated behaviours as listed in the previous section and the appendix, you will see that making, identifying and applying concepts from apparently unrelated experiences forms part of the 'Using Intellect to Optimize Results' cluster of the MCI Personal Competence Model.

Use the scenario as a starting point for how you think and react to situations. Not only should you consider how the characters react but how you would react in the particular situation. Then you should transfer that situation into your own environment, both in terms of past events and possible future ones.

Liz, as we discovered at the beginning of the book, was promoted from a city-centre branch of her travel agency firm to be the deputy manager in a smaller suburban branch.

The branch that she joined was part of a family group of three travel agencies that had been owned by the same family for nearly 25 years, starting with one small outlet. The family had given up most of the day-to-day control about eight years ago, and her manager, John, had then looked after all three branches in a general manager role. Following family retirements, younger members found that they had little interest in the business. As competition from national chains of travel agents was increasing, they decided to sell the business to one of the major national operators.

This occurred three years ago. The new owners closed two of the three branches almost immediately, as the chain had established branches fairly nearby. John had been kept on but now only managed the one branch.

THINK POINT

If you were John, what might your feelings be about this apparent demotion, and how might his situation have been viewed by his family, friends and colleagues?

We will be seeing how the takeover has affected John. There is no doubt that he could be demotivated in terms of career development. His employers have recognized that he may have been feeling a lack of status, and have recently asked him to act as the area's business travel consultant – a field in which he has little experience, but one in which senior management think he will excel. This had led to Liz's appointment as deputy manager. This is a new post; the previous branch structure, in all suburban branches, being a manager plus a group of travel consultants, one of whom was designated as a senior travel consultant and who stood in for the manager during his or her absence. City-centre branches have both a manager and a deputy manager.

The key people you will meet in the scenario are as follows.

John – the Branch Manager

John is 52 years old and has been with the original company for 17 years and in the travel trade all his life. As stated earlier, he also has an area responsibility for business travel, a field of work in which he has not had very much prior experience. Whilst his employers see this as a challenge, he see it very much as a threat. Not a particularly sociable man, he is uncomfortable with some of the social aspects of this role, although the fact that he is a keen golfer helps in that he can take clients out for a game.

His wife Eileen was recently made redundant from her secretarial job, and with their two children, Robin (18) and Samantha (21) both at university, money is an issue. He is determined to hang on to his job (even though he is not happy) until he no longer has any financial responsibilities for them.

He has few formal qualifications and feels threatened by 'high-flyers' such as Liz and the Area Manager, Simon. He did not approve of Liz's appointment as he didn't feel the need for a deputy manager, and was concerned that she was too young and thus might lack experience. He was overruled by Simon, the Area Manager.

Of a traditional and conservative nature, he has been a Justice of the Peace (Magistrate) for 10 years. This work normally entails his absence from the branch for a day every two weeks.

Liz – the Deputy Manager

Liz is 25 years old and married to Alan (30), who runs the family building firm that he inherited from his father two years ago. The firm has had recent cash-flow problems, and thus Liz's salary is invaluable. They have no children.

Liz holds a Certificate in Travel and Tourism and has been placed on the company's NVQ4 in Management scheme as part of her development as a manager within the organization. Simon believes that she has considerable potential, hence his pressure to secure her appointment.

Her next promotion will need to be in another area of the country to fit in with company policy, and this will not suit her domestic arrangements; or she could be appointed to John's job if this became vacant.

She has now been in post for four months and was Simon's first appointment. Her husband thought that the promotion to a branch nearer home would mean that they could spend more time together, but she finds that she is having to stay on in the evenings later and later in order to carry out her administrative tasks, as John is doing more JP work and is out seeing business travel clients on a more regular basis.

Her interests include travel, but although she can obtain discounted tickets Alan finds it difficult to leave his business. Liz is also becoming interested in foreign languages because she sees this as a way of enhancing her role within the organization. She is currently studying Spanish at evening classes.

Jason – Travel Consultant

Jason is 19 and in his first job. He has been in the branch for two years. He hasn't given much thought to his career in the past, and most of his energies have been devoted to the local Sunday league football club for whom he captains a team.

He has, however, recently become engaged to Paula, a receptionist in a local surgery, and he is now more aware of his need to progress because they are keen to buy a house.

His main area of work involves domestic travel arrangements, a job that he finds rather boring and repetitive.

Sue – Travel Consultant

Sue (36) has been with the branch for 18 months. She has returned to work after her children started school, having been a machinist in a knitwear factory before they were born.

Her husband, Tony, is a machine operator in a light engineering factory and works on a shift basis.

When she started this was a convenient job near to home; but after initial training she has discovered that she really enjoys her work and is now keen to develop and progress.

Helen – Travel Consultant

Helen (24) joined the original company straight from school. She has one 'A' level, and decided to opt for a job instead of further study. She thought that working in the travel business would be exciting and glamorous. She doesn't know what she wants to do with her life. She enjoys dancing and socializing, and she and her boyfriend Mike often socialize with Claire (whom we shall meet later) and her partner.

Simon – Area Manager

Thirty-five years old and heading for the top. Simon was recruited to the chain at the time of the takeover and was appointed Area Manager six months ago, his previous post having been in head office. Liz is his first managerial appointment.

With a BA degree he is bright but has no formal management qualifications and tends to adopt an autocratic style. He has been accused (especially by John) of being brash and arrogant.

Simon is already looking for the next promotion.

He was divorced two years ago, his ex-wife claiming that the job always came first. He is very bitter, especially about the amount he has to pay out in maintenance. He has a son (12), who lives with his ex-wife and attends a rather expensive private day school.

Claire – Customer

Helen's best friend Claire is 26 and is a personnel assistant at a large local manufacturing firm. One of her tasks is to make the travel arrangements for the sales force. Being a major exporter this means that she has to arrange a great deal of foreign travel. She holds a 'Certificate in Personnel Practice' (CPP).

She is due to marry her partner Scott in six months' time.

Those are the main characters in the scenario. They are all at different points on their journeys to success; some are starting careers, some coming to the end of them; some have been in long-term relationships, for others their current relationships are very new. Simon has a clear route planned, Helen doesn't know where she wants to go. Just as this book will have readers at different stages, so are the staff of this travel agency. In the pages that follow you are invited to see how their personal competence develops, to see how they grow and then reflect on your own growth and development.

Each section contains cases based on this scenario that present different issues and problems. Techniques and concepts to assist are then considered in the light of the situation, possible solutions are analysed, and you are then asked to complete the relevant section of your personal action plan in chapter 10.

2
Where am I Now?

It was coming up to the annual appraisals. *Simon* would be carrying out *John's* appraisal and John in turn would be appraising *Liz*.

The organization's policy was that staff completed an appraisal form indicating their view of their performance over the last six months, two weeks before their view of the performance over the last six months, two weeks before their appraisal interview. Their manager completed a similar form on his or her perception of how the staff member had performed.

By coincidence both John and Liz were discussing one particular question with their partners.

'I always have trouble with this one – where do you want your career to be in five years' time,' John remarked to his wife Eileen. 'If I answer truthfully, I'll be hoping for early retirement. I'll be 57 then and young enough to enjoy some leisure time and perhaps a part-time job, but I can't put that down. I'll have to put that I hope for some more responsibility, but I wish I could be honest.'

'I don't know', Liz told Alan, her husband, 'In five years' time I want to be the manager of the branch, I wonder what John would say if I put that?'

'You don't know', replied Alan, 'he might approve.'

John might well approve given that he will be looking for early retirement in five years. At least that is his view now. If there are changes at work or home, his plans might change.

Before one can plan any journey, be it a career journey, a trip to the supermarket or a holiday trip, it is necessary to consider one's starting point. Many times this happens automatically: you know the way from home to the shops and yet your brain, in planning your journey, has to make a quick scan of your current surroundings so that it can work with the correct data and pull the appropriate model from your memory.

When considering personal development and competence it is vital that you consider not only where you want to go but also both where you are at the moment and where you have come from.

THINK POINT

You will be writing this down later on, but for now, where do *you* want to be in five years' time?

The characters in our scenario are at a fixed point in time and in a fixed geographical location and these factors will form part of their analysis.

The geographical location is very important to Liz as her room for manœuvre in her job is constrained by the nature of her husband's business. In John's case, time (i.e. his age) may well be an important factor, as he is between 8 and 13 years off retirement (depending on whether he retires at 60 or 65).

Under normal circumstances, Liz could expect to be a deputy manager for between two and three years before being promoted, provided she has been successful, to a branch manager position. The more successful she is, the more likely and the earlier her promotion, and this is causing a problem.

As mentioned in the scenario chapter, Alan, her husband, had hoped to see more of her when she moved to the branch, but she has been working long hours. Simon, the area manager, has already noted her dedication and has hinted that she is well on the road to a manager's position.

Liz is ambitious but the promotion will mean that, in all probability, she would have to move to another part of the country, unless John's position became vacant.

As her husband is running the family building firm, a move for him would be impossible. So is the promotion desirable and if not, he wonders, 'why is she working so hard and putting in all the extra hours?'

John has a different set of concerns. He is happy as he is and doesn't really want the extra responsibilities of looking after business travel. He will retire as soon as he is offered a suitable financial package; so why should he expand extra energy developing new business? And yet he does.

For both these individuals there is a need to look at where they want to go, and to perform those analyses they need to consider how they have arrived at the present position. In order to do this, it is necessary to perform a series of three analyses known respectively as BACK, PEST and SWOT analyses. At the end of the chapter you will be asked to perform and record the same analyses on yourself in order to start your journey to success.

BACK ANALYSIS

A back analysis is concerned with those factors that have been involved with a person reaching a specific point in their personal journey. The letters stand for:

Baggage
Aspirations
Culture
Knowledge

Baggage

We all carry with us a degree of 'baggage' that we have picked up along our journey. Human beings seem better at collecting baggage as opposed to discarding it, and so the amount of baggage we carry with us seems to grow from year to year.

Baggage is those things that have shaped the way we think as an individual, and it relates closely to our life experiences. Social class, family relationships, friendships and good or bad experiences all form part of our collected baggage. Baggage is important because the way we behave in the future will be largely determined by the experiences we have had in the past. Lou Tice (1989) in the USA has coined the term 'comfort zones' to describe the areas of life in which we feel most at home. We are in our comfort zone when the world we live in matches our perception of our place within the world.

This concept begins to explain why those who win enormous sums on the football pools and the National Lottery often find that this brings them great unhappiness as it moves them outside their current comfort zone by a large amount. Tice's work has shown that in such a situation people subconsciously try to move back to their comfort zone.

Whilst some books on personal development will advise you that you can do anything you want if you want it badly enough, experience and common sense suggests that our future plans will be affected by what has gone before, that is, by the baggage we bring with us. Liz's future cannot help be affected by the decisions she and her husband have made in the past. She could work anywhere, but this would probably be at the expense of her marriage, a price most people would be very unwilling to pay. Movement through your 'comfort zone' will be discussed in chapter 3 of this book when we examine change.

Inside our memories we carry everything that has happened to us; this is our 'baggage'. If we have had a pleasant experience we will want to repeat it: if a bad experience, we want to avoid a repetition or even the danger of a repetition. This is why it is sometimes hard to start driving again after a car accident. We know that 'lightning rarely strikes twice in the same place', but subconsciously we don't want to take even the smallest risk of a repetition. As time goes on, the less likely it is we will drive again.

Aspirations

If baggage is about the past, aspirations are about the future. Aspirations are what we want to do. It might be argued that dreams are about our plans for the future; for the purpose of this book, aspirations can be described as attainable dreams. As mentioned in the previous chapter, baggage from the past will affect what can be done in the future. Aspirations are dreams and plans that take this baggage (plus factors from our next two areas, Culture and Knowledge) into account, and that is why they form part of the 'Where am I now?' analysis.

Whilst aspirations should be personal, i.e. what you want, it is impossible not to take account of the aspirations others – family, friends, colleagues, employers, and so forth – may have for you. Sometimes these will conflict and you will have to decide who you are going to please. Experience shows that if we put the aspirations others have for us before those we have for ourselves, frustration and failure are often the result. You need ownership of aspirations. Many parents have pushed their children on courses in life that met the parent's aspirations for the child and not the child's own aspirations. The same parents were often dismayed when rebellion occurred and the child went their own way. Only you can aspire for you: others can advise or guide, but the ultimate decisions are yours.

Jason may well have dreams to become a professional foot-baller and to play for a Premier Division side; however, unless he has the necessary skills and physical abilities this will remain a dream, it cannot become an aspiration. Even if all the necessary requirements are in place, aspirations will remain unfulfilled unless a person makes the necessary steps to ensure that they bring themselves to the notice of those making appointments, and are prepared to compromise other areas of their lives as we have seen with Liz.

Unless you are prepared to realize that not all dreams are realistically fulfillable, frustration can set in. Having decided where you want to go, you need to ensure that the baggage you take with you will be useful and relevant.

Using Liz as an example, her aspirations need to take account of the problems that moving away from home would cause. If she wants promotion badly enough, then compromises within her domestic situation and within her husband's work situation will need to be made.

Culture

Culture was mentioned in the introduction to this book. Culture can be described as an individual's, a group's, a society's or even a nation's *values*, *attitudes* and *beliefs*. Culture becomes engrained at a very early age. For individuals, the vast majority of their cultural baggage (for culture is very much part of the baggage we carry around with us) is part of a collective set of values, attitudes and beliefs. We share these with those we tend to associate with, and they become the way we do things around here, as examined in the preface.

Whilst it may require some soul searching to critically examine one's basic beliefs, it is important. You will be unlikely to take steps in the future if they conflict with your cultural norms. As organizations have their own cultural norms, it is important that people try to seek employment with those organizations, which if they have cultural norms, are acceptable to the employees' personal culture, or at least not in violent conflict with it.

The growth in 'ethical' shareholding in the 1990s – where investors will not put money into companies that have environmental, employment or political (political in the sense of countries where they operate) operations with which they disagree – is an example of people trying to balance their personal cultural norms with those of the organizations they are involved with.

Much frustration at work may be due to a basic clash between personal and organizational culture. In the UK, the 1990s saw major cultural changes in the way local government organizations were structured and carried out their business. Many employees, who had joined local government because the ideals of local democracy were in tune with their personal beliefs, became very uncomfortable with the changes, and many left. This was very noticeable in the teaching profession, where a large number of headteachers sought early retirement after the introduction of local management of schools which forced them to become business managers rather than teachers *per se*. A similar situation has developed within the National Health Service.

In John's case, the culture he had been working in for 17 years had been that of a small family business. Such a business would have had a certain set of values, attitudes and beliefs, probably quite traditional. He is now working for a large national organization. His greatest problem probably will not have been the functional tasks he has been required to carry out but the change in culture, the change in his way of thinking or mind-set. We shall examine how to cope with these types of changes in the next chapter.

Knowledge

The final factor in the BACK analysis concerns the knowledge, skills and aptitudes you have acquired on your journey through life up to this point. They too have a connection with baggage; indeed a BACK analysis model could be presented as shown in figure 4.

In the short term, your plans will have to be accomplished with the knowledge and skills you already have. It takes time to learn new ones, and so they form another important part of the baggage you bring with you, as indeed does any lack of knowledge or skills.

By completing a formal skills check or skills scan, often used in management development programmes and linked to special areas of competence, gaps can be identified and training and learning plans developed.

John, as we know from the scenario, has little experience of business travel, and yet this is becoming an important part of his work. If he analyses what he does know and what he needs to know, this will identify the training gap (see *In Charge, Managing People*, chapter 7, for more details), and he can then plan actions to minimize the gap, through courses, seminars, reading, etc.

A BACK analysis is the first step in considering where you are. You should now turn to the back of this volume to complete your

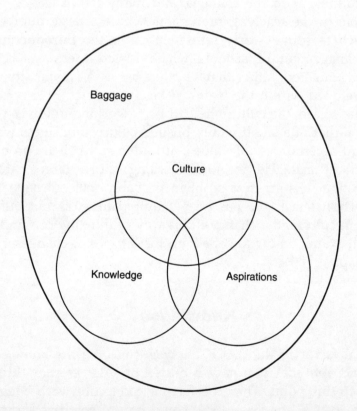

Figure 4 The BACK analysis model

personal BACK analysis based on your *baggage* including your current comfort zone, your *aspirations*.

Please note: you may not be used to writing in books (indeed a reluctance to do so may be considered as an example of *baggage*) but the Action Plan is there for you to put your ideas and thoughts down on paper. It will build up into a very useful document for your personal use. Please use it.

ACTION PLAN 1

Turn to your Action Plan at the end of the book (chapter 10). If you need ideas, an abbreviated version of this part of an action plan for John is included at the end of this chapter. The first section is labelled 'Baggage' followed by 'Current Comfort Zone'. Look at the categories and write a brief description of where you are now. The headings are: *home, job, family* and *money*. For each category you need to be very honest about the zone in which you feel comfortable. If you earn £12,000 p.a., your comfort zone is probably £10,000–£15,000 p.a., below £10,000 you would find it difficult to maintain your current lifestyle, above £15,000 you might find that you feel uncomfortable because of society's expectations and your own unease about moving away too far, too quickly from your current position. If this sounds paradoxical, consider what would happen if Liz received an immediate large rise: would it make Alan and her lives that much better, or might he feel resentful and might she feel the need to work even harder to justify the extra pay? You need to consider these matters very carefully. After the Comfort Zone section are sections for Aspirations, Culture and Knowledge.

What you have been considering is a profile of you as a person. You also need to consider the type of person you are – your personality. Certain types of jobs and activities suit one more than the other. There are a number of personality tests on the market and a detailed consideration is beyond the scope of this book. One concept, however, that the authors have used with considerable success with both individuals and work groups relates to the idea of 'team roles' as developed by Meredith Belbin. This is most appropriate, as your journey to success will not be accomplished on your own but in association with others, the groups and teams with whom you live and work.

Team roles were covered in detail in chapter 8 of *In Charge, Managing People*, and the relevant section of that chapter is adapted and repeated here.

THE CONCEPT OF TEAM ROLES

Buchanan and Huczynski (1985) considered that the structure of a group can be differentiated in the following ways: *liking*, *status*, *power*, *leadership* and *role*; and it is on the latter that the next section of this chapter centres. They also noted the fact that as regards roles, most people have in fact two roles within a group: the role they perceive that they should have, and the role that they actually enact; Belbin's work (1981), which is discussed next, attempts to encourage convergence between the two and also looks at the difference between the functional role within a group that members are allocated and the more personality-based team role that they adopt naturally.

Team roles are described by Belbin (1981: 169) as:

> a pattern of behaviour characteristic of the way in which one team member interacts with another where his performance serves to facilitate the progress of the team as a whole.

We are all members of teams, be it at home, work or in our social interactions.

The work of Meredith Belbin, initially at the Henley Management Centre and latterly in Cambridge, has provided a clearer insight into internal group relationships and clarification of the roles needed for a team or group to work effectively.

Belbin's work with a large number of individuals suggested that there are nine possible team roles that a person can adopt. Some are natural roles, some are roles that a person can adopt if necessary and some are roles that the person finds very hard to adopt. Other work, such as that carried out by Margerison and McCann (1985), has come up with very similar findings.

The team types Belbin postulated are as follows:

(PL)	Plant:	Very creative, the ideas person
(RI)	Resource Investigator:	Extrovert, good at making outside contracts and developing ideas
(ME)	Monitor Evaluator:	Shrewd and prudent, analytical
(SH)	Shaper:	Dynamic and challenging
(CO)	Co-ordinator:	Respected, mature and good at ensuring that talents are used effectively
(IMP)	Implementor:	Practical, loyal and task orientated
(CF)	Completer Finisher	Meticulous and attentive to detail
(TW)	Teamworker:	Caring and very person oriented
(SP)	Specialist:	High technical skill, and professional as opposed to organizational prime loyalties

For each of the team role 'strengths' quoted above, Belbin considered that there were allowable weaknesses, the price that had to be paid for the strength.

The allowable weakness postulated by Belbin are:

(PL)	Plant:	Weak in communicating with and managing ordinary people
(RI)	Resource Investigator:	Easily bored after the initial enthusiasm has passed
(ME)	Monitor Evaluator:	Lacks drive and ability to inspire others
(SH)	Shaper:	Prone to provocation and bursts of temper
(CO)	Co-ordinator:	Not necessarily the most clever or creative member of the group
(IMP)	Implementor:	Inflexible and slow to respond to new opportunities
(CF)	Completer Finisher:	Inclined to worry and reluctant to delegate
(TW)	Teamworker:	Indecisive in crunch situations
(SP)	Specialist:	Contributes on only a narrow front

It is dangerous to treat the allowable weaknesses as areas to be removed; to do so might also involve losing the underlying strength. Rather, the weaknesses need to be managed and understood.

Research using the Belbin concepts has shown that having a language to describe strengths and weaknesses in this way allows groups/team members to understand each other, and aids the work process.

THINK POINT

What do you believe are your preferred team roles? How well-balanced is your team – are there any gaps that need filling?

Look at the members of your work group/team: which are their preferred team roles and which roles should they avoid?

Think about famous people: what roles did they prefer? Make a list. Here are some ideas to start you off:

Plant   Clive Sinclair
Shaper   Margaret Thatcher
Co-ordinator   John Major

ACTION PLAN 2

Now complete the Team Role section of the action plan at the end of the book.

If we were to consider the characters in our scenario in Belbin team-role terms, it would be likely that John would score highly as a monitor evaluator/implementor; Helen would be an implementor/teamworker; Liz shows definite shaper and plant tendencies; and Simon appears to be a strong shaper. As you read through the volume you might like to ascribe such preferred team roles to the other characters. Later in the book we will consider how the characters' team-role profiles might appear.

All those who have written on teamwork have stressed the need for a balance or blend of team members. Belbin himself stresses the need for balance, and this is echoed by writers such as McGregor (1960), who wrote of the need for a balance of roles within managerial teams. McGregor was concerned that the creative (*plant* in Belbin terms) and dynamic (*shaper* in Belbin terms) roles should be counterbalanced by a critical thinking (*monitor evaluator* in Belbin terms) role within the team. In order to test for team-role types, Belbin developed the 'Interplace' computer program, which produces a profile and a series of reports. Interplace is marketed as a recruitment aid, as are other tests such as 16PF and OPQ, which use similar terms to Interplace to describe team roles. Belbin's research showed that effective teams were comprised of between five to seven members and contained a blend of team-role types. As there are nine team-role types, people need to use more than one type. For example, a person may act as a *plant* at the beginning of a project but as a *specialist* later on. Teams containing members who all had high team-role scores (Apollo Teams) were not especially effective and teams containing only two or three roles were very ineffective. A team of *plants* might be very creative but would be unlikely to implement the ideas. Conversely a team of *implementors* might be very practical but would lack the creativity to break new ground.

In his orginal work, Belbin used the terms 'Chairman' (CH) instead of *co-ordinator*, and 'Company Worker' (CW) instead of *implementor*. The role of *specialist* is a later addition and does not figure in the original research.

Generalizing about team roles, Buchanan and Huczynski split them up into two main sections, task roles and maintenance roles. The task roles were: initiator, information seeker, diagnoser, opinion seeker, evaluator and decision manager; whereas the maintenance functions were: encourager, compromiser, peace-keeper, clarifier, summarizer, standard setter. These categories can be easily equated with the Belbin team roles. If certain team roles predominate in a particular professional/occupational group, then there is the danger that any team formed from members of that group will not function as effectively as possible. Eleven centre-forwards may have considerable collective talent but are unlikely to perform as well as a team containing a goalkeeper, defenders, middle players, etc. Similarly, a work team with too many *plants* may produce too many conflicting ideas with a lack of follow through. The research set out to look for such imbalance, and the following chapters show the results of the research, areas for those involved in team building in the work situation to consider, and possible future areas of research.

When recruiting new members to a group/team, the supervisor/first-line manager should consider not only the tasks that the person will be carrying out but also the roles present within the group/team and the type of roles the applicant has as natural roles.

For further information and examples of the types of tests you might want to try, you are advised to read *Test Your Own Aptitude* by J. Barrett and G. Williams. You will learn more about your preferred learning style in chapter 4 of this volume.

PEST ANALYSIS

The BACK analysis is basically about yourself. The PEST analysis is about the world that you live in. Normally used as part of an organizational analysis, the concept of a PEST analysis is amended here in order to assist you in considering those factors outside your control that will influence your development and future decisions. A PEST analysis is a technique for scanning the environment that you live and work in in order to focus on key external factors.

The letters stand for:

Political
Economic
Social
Technological

Political

The word *political* may cause you some problems, but it is not related to the party you support but rather to effects that official bodies – international, national, local and professional, not forgetting your employers – might have on your development. Using Liz as an example, the fact that she is undertaking an

NVQ4 in Management qualification means that any changes the government makes in grants for vocational changes, etc. are likely to affect her. This would be a political factor. Similarly, for newly engaged Jason, any further changes in the policies for interest relief for homeowners will be a political factor even if the effects may be economic. The decision to close two branches would have been a political factor affecting John's development.

Internal office politics may well be an issue you wish to consider here. You will meet examples of office politics in the scenario firm later in the book.

For different people there will be different factors. You need to look at your situation and consider what measures the European Commission, the government, your local council, your professional association or trade union and your employers are involved in at the moment (or in the very near future); and then ensure that what you want will not be hindered by them – or, as we shall see in the next section on strengths and weaknesses, what you can do to exploit or to mitigate against them.

The same applies to the other factors. *Economic* factors include rates of pay, interest rates, cost of living and items of expenditure you cannot avoid. John has two children at university and his wife has recently been made redundant. His children in this instance and at this particular moment in time are an economic factor.

Social factors relate to areas in which social change may affect you. Green issues, changes in work patterns (such as the growth in part-time work) and educational trends come under this heading. Again, the actual items will be different for each individual. You need to ask yourself, what is happening in society that is likely to affect my development now or in the near future? And again, is this an opportunity I must grasp or a threat I must mitigate against?

Technological advances since World War II have been tremendous. In 1980 nobody had heard of the facsimile (fax) machine; by 1990 they were in common use; by 1994 people were installing them at home as well as in the office. This area of the PEST analysis requires you to consider technological aspects that will be affecting you.

None of these areas can be pigeon-holed discretely – they overlap. Political factors may spill over into the economic, a change in technology may affect the way society views things, but completing a PEST analysis gives you a good view of the world in which your development must take place.

ACTION PLAN 3

Turn again to the action plan at the end of the book (chapter 10). If you need assistance, an abbreviated version of this part of the action plan is included for Liz at the end of this chapter.

   You should perform a PEST analysis on your situation, using the political, economic, social and technological headings included in the blank plan.

As a result of the action plans you have completed so far you will have produced a picture of yourself and a picture of the world you live and work in. The next step is to use each of these to produce a SWOT analysis.

SWOT

A SWOT analysis (sometimes referred to as an OTWS or 'Otherwise' analysis from the phrase in *In Charge, Managing Operations*: 'Organizations must carry out this analysis OTHERWISE they go out of business') stands for:

Strengths
Weaknesses
Opportunities
Threats

Strengths and weaknesses are internal, they are *your* strengths and weaknesses. They are those things you excel at and those things that you are not as good at. Again, they will be different for each individual. They will be derived from your BACK analysis and you can use the aspirations section of that analysis to filter out irrelevant items. If you don't want to be a footballer, having two left feet may be a weakness but it is an irrelevant one. In Jason's case, of course, it may be very relevant.

Opportunities and threats come from outside and are generated from your PEST analysis.

In the case of strengths and weaknesses, an item could appear under both headings. Not being afraid to speak your mind may be both a strength and a weakness in the same person. You must decide where the balance will lie.

Similarly, one person's threat is another's opportunity. An organizational review may be a threat to John but Liz may see it as an advantage.

THINK POINT

If the headquarters of the scenario firm decided to re-organize their branches, what threats might this pose to John and what opportunities for Liz? You also need to consider whether there are opportunities for John and any threats to Liz.

Whenever you undertake this analysis be careful to consider whether there could be a threat lurking within an apparent opportunity; and can you convert, by your own actions, a threat to an opportunity. A takeover by a German firm might be considered a threat by our scenario characters. Were Liz to add German lessons to the ones she is already taking in Spanish, she could turn this into a personal opportunity.

ACTION PLAN 4

Carrying on your action plan at the end of the book, you now need to perform a personal SWOT analysis. To help you, an abbreviated SWOT analysis for John is included at the end of this chapter.

Having considered where you are, the next chapter will look at where you might want to go on your 'Journey to success'.

As you have seen in the action plan you have been asked to complete, a SWOT analysis is usually carried out on quartered paper (see figure 5).

| Strengths | Weaknesses |
| Opportunities | Threats |

Figure 5 A SWOT analysis

SUMMARY

This chapter has concentrated on three types of analysis to help determine your current position.

The information about you; your BACK (Baggage, Aspirations, Culture and Knowledge) analysis and a PEST (Political, Economic, Social and Technological) analysis combined to form a SWOT (Strengths, Weaknesses, Opportunities and Threats) analysis.

Remember that these apply only to you and your situation.

Only by analysing where you are and where you've come from can you begin to plan where you want to go to.

Example analyses

For the first two chapters only, we are giving simplified examples of how the action plans could be completed for some of the people in the scenario. Your action plan will need more detail.

BACK ANALYSIS FOR JOHN

a1) *Baggage*

What events in the past have most influenced where you are, what you do and who you're with now? List the most important.

Fear of redundancy during takeover
Family commitments
Mortgage
Parents wish for him to have a professional career

a2) *Comfort zone*

Write a brief description of your current comfort zone under the following headings:

Home
Detached house, 2 bathrooms, greenhouse, large kitchen

Job
Secure, white-collar, managerial, in charge of staff, near home

Family
Stable, support for children, care of older relatives; children with degrees

Money
£18,000–£22,000 p.a., second salary of at least £10,000 p.a.

b) *Aspirations*

Being realistic what do you want to be doing:

One year from now?
Secure in the same branch but with extra staff and some extra responsibilities

Five years from now?

Taking early retirement [we said 'be honest']

Ten years from now?
In a bungalow on the South Coast

Are there any aspirations others have for you? List them plus your feelings about them.

My family would like to see me becoming an Area Manager but I'd like a quiet life [honesty again].

c) *Culture*

Culture can be defined in terms of *values*, *attitudes* and *beliefs*. In a few sentences for each, try to analyse these in terms of your personal:

VALUES

> *Family ties are important*
> *Traditional values are slipping*
> *Honesty and integrity in business dealings*

ATTITUDES

> *I am the breadwinner*
> *Hard work brings respect*
> *I treat people as I would want them to treat me*
> *Seniority brings respect*

BELIEFS

> *Families come first*
> *Loyalty is its own reward*
> *Traditional ways still have a place*

(You may not agree with all of these, but read the scenario about John again – is this how he might think?)

d) *Knowledge*

List below, first, any special qualifications you may hold; then skills you believe that you can demonstrate competence in; and finally, any special aptitudes you believe you have.

QUALIFICATIONS

4 'O' Levels
Fares and booking qualifications

SKILLS

People management
Computer literacy

APTITUDES

Getting the best out of people
Sport (golf)

TEAM ROLES for John

Co-ordinator
Teamworker
Monitor Evaluator

PEST ANALYSIS FOR LIZ

POLITICAL

Easier border controls within the European Union
H2 policy on management development
Acceptability of NV2s

ECONOMIC

Recession – affecting people's holiday and travel plans
Husband's business

SOCIAL

More people holidaying abroad
Move towards more women in senior management

TECHNOLOGICAL

Language training
Computerized booking systems

SWOT ANALYSIS FOR JOHN

STRENGTHS	WEAKNESSES
Years in the trade	Slow to change
Knowledge of countries	Traditional
Respected	Resentment of Liz
OPPORTUNITIES	THREATS
Business travel	Liz and Simon
Expansion	Business travel
	New technology

(Remember, items can be both opportunities and threats.)

3
Where do I Want to Get to, and How am I Going to Get There?

Having established where you are, it is now time to look at where you wish to go and the way you will travel to your destination.

The chapter is split up into a number of sections:

What do you know about your destination?
What personal plans do you have?
The management of change
Positive thinking
Planning
Excellence

Each section includes case notes based on the scenario and an example of action plans based on the characters.

WHAT DO YOU KNOW ABOUT YOUR DESTINATION?

The very fact that you are reading this book indicates that you have some ideas about where you want your life to lead you. In the action planning for the last section you considered your present position together with a look at your aspirations.

Turn to the aspirations section of your action plan and remind yourself of your aspirations.

THINK POINT

Do some of your aspirations seem too remote or too difficult to achieve? If so, can you 'break up' the journey and consider more obtainable aspirations that will still be on the road to your ultimate goal?

Hastings et al., in their book *Superteams* (1986), coined the phrase 'milestones not millstones'. If you set yourself goals, targets and aspirations that are too remote or too difficult, they become a millstone around your neck. Whilst never losing sight of your ultimate destination, you need a series of milestones along the way. Just as many motorists use motorway service areas not only for rest but as markers to show how far they have travelled, and perhaps more importantly, how far they still have to go, so you need a series of aspirations that will allow you to taste success at frequent intervals and to provide a guide as to how you are doing. We will consider monitoring your progress in later chapters.

THINK POINT

In your action plan, you wrote down where you wanted to be one year, five years and ten years from now. Check what you wrote and make sure that the three responses lie on the same 'road'. The one-year response should be a milestone on the way to the five-year response, etc. If this isn't so, think again!

When you are thinking about your future destination, be sure that you really want to end up there. If you complete your action plan and use the concepts in this book, you are more than likely to achieve what you want. You need to be very careful, therefore, that you really do want to achieve it, as there is nothing worse than making a long journey only to find that you would rather be somewhere else.

Just as the SWOT analysis you completed in the last section forced you to look at your weaknesses as well as your strengths, you need to consider your destination in terms of possible drawbacks as well as the good things you will achieve.

THINK POINT

Was it easier to consider your strengths or your weaknesses when you completed your action plan? We will consider this question again when we examine the concept of 'positive thinking'.

Simon was on a routine visit to the branch. He'd just finished talking to the staff, as he always did on visits. Simon was very proud of his 'people skills' and he'd read all about the concept of 'Management by Wandering Around' (MBWA) (Peters 1988). The concept suggests that good managers can only find out about what is happening – and, most importantly, what people feel about issues – by being visible and practising active listening skills. He'd just finished talking to Sue and Helen.

'There's a man who knows where he's going,' remarked Sue. 'Well I wish I did,' replied Helen; and to Sue's quizzical look she began to expand on her frustrations.

Helen had left school at 18 having gained one 'A' level and having made the decision to stop studying and take up a job. Not a *career*, because she had no idea what she wanted to do. She had entered the travel agency business because she thought that it would be glamorous, but it was the customers who went to all the exotic places, not her. True, she could obtain some discounts. But her boyfriend, Mike, couldn't always take time off from work. She felt in a rut; and to make things worse, her best friend, Claire, seemed to be really enjoying her job and had the next few years mapped out. Even Sue, who had come back into work after her children started school, was really becoming excited by the job and was looking for extra training and responsibility.

'Simon knows where he's going, Claire knows, you know,' she complained to Sue. . . . 'But what about me?'

Helen isn't alone, although the presumption that it's only younger people who don't know where they're going is not true. Many people have successful career changes in later life.

In order to understand about your destination, you have to begin to determine where it is. This has to be done carefully. If you have too broad an idea, you will have no focus for your ambitions. Too precise a destination and you may neglect useful, related alternatives.

A sensible suggestion is to think of your journey as a funnel (figure 6). As you proceed along the journey, your ideas about your destination become more focused. Your knowledge about potential destinations also becomes greater, enabling you to make better informed choices.

In this way, if Helen wants to work in the travel business but would like more excitement, all is not lost. The work that she has done at the travel agency will aid her knowledge of the industry and allow her to focus her ideas more closely. Build up your knowledge and check that you are still inside the funnel and, of course, you should make sure that your destination should be

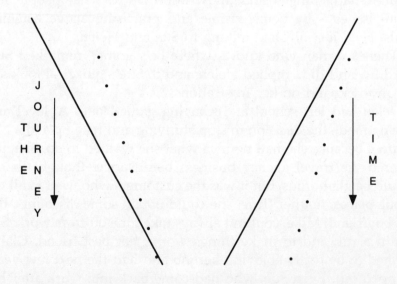

Figure 6 Funnel focus

compatible with the analyses you carried out in the last chapter.

WHAT ARE MY PERSONAL PLANS?

In the next chapter you will be examining conflict. One source of conflict occurs when personal plans conflict with the plans of your colleagues and your organization.

If we believe that somebody is making our decisions for us we often become very angry. One answer is to make sure that you know what your plans are and to let others know what you want. Appraisal interviews, career counselling and even recruitment interviews provide a vehicle for you to do this. You need to ensure, however, that you are clear in your mind about what you want, and if you change your plans, let people know. Provided you are realistic and talking about the 'milestones' we mentioned earlier, people will accept this.

'I'm sorry John, but I've had arrangements made for tomorrow for weeks. Saturdays off are very precious and we're planning to spend the day with friends.' The atmosphere in John's office was becoming tense. One of Sue's children had to go into hospital for a minor operation and John was trying to persuade Helen to work an extra Saturday to cover for Sue whilst she was at the hospital.

'It's one of our busiest days and I need you here,' John was becoming tetchy.

'Well this firm doesn't own me, it's my day off and Claire and I have plans. She puts a lot of business our way for her company, I wonder what she'd think of your bullying.'

'I wasn't bullying, I just need you here to help . . .'

Helen is involved in a short-term example of a conflict of plans. It would be good for her career to help but possibly bad for her social relationships.

A successful journey through life is about balancing our personal plans with the plans of others and the plans they may have for us.

Liz didn't know it, but Simon had long-term plans for her career. He wanted to see her as a manager. True, Liz wanted that, but her plans didn't involve her moving far away; Simon believed that she should take a position anywhere within reason. They hadn't discussed it yet, but it would come up one day.

THINK POINT

Has somebody ever had plans for you that didn't match up with your personal plans? How did you react?

We will examine the planning process later in this chapter.

MANAGING CHANGE

Life is not constant. Very few things remain unchanged for long. One has only to look at the advances in communications technology in the past few years to realize how fast and how significant the changes have been.

Sue and Helen were discussing the new instructions about holidays that Simon had left during his visit.

'I don't like this new arrangement, it seems that it only suits the bosses,' Helen was not happy.

'But you've been saying for ages that you'd like a more flexible arrangement. It suits me as I can fit it in around the childrens' holidays. Anyway they asked for ideas from us, did you put any in?'

'No, of course not, but I don't like the way they've done this. I don't know why they need to change things around anyway.'

Whilst we may often yearn for change, when it comes we are not so sure; perhaps what we had before wasn't so bad after all. We know what the *present* is like, whereas the *future* is somewhat unknown.

This indeed is part of the theory behind the comfort zone concept postulated by Tice and mentioned in chapter 2 and later in this book. Even though it may not be a perfect situation, we are comfortable with what we know and may be reluctant to change even though we are promised that things will be better.

Kurt Lewin (1951), an American, has developed an interesting way of looking at change, that many supervisors/first-line

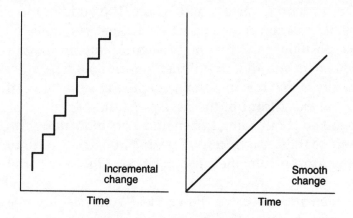

Figure 7 Incremental and smooth change

managers have found extremely useful when required to implement organizational changes.

Lewin's concept was that although change can be planned, the outcome is never certain. Were change incremental (in small planned steps) or smooth (e.g. figure 7), then life would be simple, changes would be small and non-threatening. However, the reality is more like figure 8.

Real change, i.e. change in the real world, involves rapid movement from a stable position to a new position which then stabilizes before the next rapid movement. The reasons for the change are often external and may include product changes,

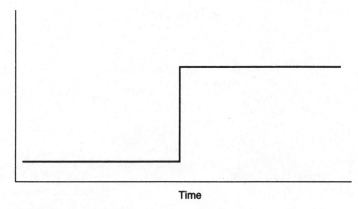

Figure 8 Real change

legislation, economic factors and so on. The sudden movement from a stable position can be very threatening. The concept is that the stable position must first be broken up into an unstructured amorphous one, and that it will then reform into a new position. The difficulty is that it is impossible to predict with a great deal of accuracy the exact form of the new position.

Lewin talked about being frozen into a position, unfreezing, the uncertainty that this produces, refreezing into a new position, and then being frozen into the new position. This is illustrated in figure 9.

Lewin then produced his 'Force Field Analysis' approach for dealing with changes. If you examine the way people try to implement change, they often try to overcome any resistance by pushing harder.

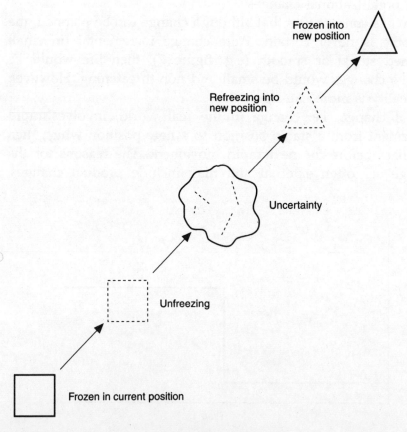

Figure 9 Unfreezing and refreezing

THINK POINT

This is a think point that requires some physical action. Ask somebody to hold out their hand to you with their palm at right angles to their arm. You do the same and place your palm over theirs and push (gently!). What do they do? In all probability they will push back.

Newton's Third Law of Motion is that for every action there is an equal and opposite reaction. The harder you push, the more resistance you are likely to encounter, unless you have taken steps to reduce the resistance. This can be illustrated as in figure 10.

The Lewin technique suggests that you consider all the reasons for making a change, the *drivers*, and then all those reasons for holding back, the *restrainers*. You can even make them of different lengths and thicknesses on your diagram to reflect different priorities and anxieties. If, taking all factors into consideration, the *restrainers* outnumber the *drivers*, change will be uncomfortable, may have damaging effects on relationships and will require considerable energy. If, on the other hand, you can look at the *restrainers* and come up with strategies to remove fears and anxieties, then the change will occur with relatively less disruption and will need less energy.

In order to carry out this analysis with success you will need to know a little about the psychological reactions to change that people, including yourself, go through.

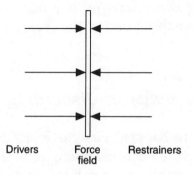

Drivers   Force   Restrainers
                 field

Figure 10 Force Field Analysis

The 'coping cycle' of Adams, Hayes and Hopson (1976) suggests that we go through five stages in our reactions to and coming to terms with change. Whilst originally postulated with the needs of organizations in mind, the cycle is equally relevant to personal change.

Stage 1: Denial

As Helen said at the beginning of this section, 'I don't know why they want to change things around anyway'. One of the first reactions to change, after the idea has had time to sink in, is to deny that there is any need for it. In Lewin and Tice terms, we are comfortable in the position we are in, and may well not wish to acknowledge the need to unfreeze. Note the use of the word 'acknowledge'; we may know full well that change is necessary, but we don't want to admit that it is; or if we do admit it, then we might not want it to go so far or in a particular direction.

Stage 2: Defence

Change means that life is going to be different. You may find yourself having to deal with new people, new ideas, new technologies, a new location. Even when you admit that the change is necessary and acknowledge it publicly, defence still occurs. You will want to maintain as much of your comfort zone as possible. Perhaps change can be just the same only better! Because you know that it is necessary and that your defence is more instinctive than rational, self-esteem can go down. You know it's a losing battle but you feel that you have to fight it. Don't worry; it's a natural part of the cycle because it leads on to the third stage.

Stage 3: Discarding

Two things begin to happen. First, as you refreeze into the new situation you begin to become more comfortable with it and, secondly, because of this, you can begin to discard any of the old ideas that you had that were acting as restrainers. An example of this can be seen when somebody moves to another part of the country. First, they try to keep up with their old friends and may not socialize much, but then they begin to make new ones in the new location. Eventually they move to Stage 4, adaptation, where their lives are adapted to keep the best of the old whilst becoming comfortable in the new.

Stage 4: Adaptation

As mentioned above, we don't discard everything from before. We adapt the best and fit it into our new situation, a situation that we have become frozen into and that leads to the final stage.

Stage 5: Internalization

When the change started, the old situation was what you were comfortable with and the new was threatening. By the time you have been through the first four stages you have reached a point where it is the new situation that you are comfortable with; you have internalized it, it is part of you. People who return to an area after a number of years or go back to a firm they were happy with are often surprised to find how uncomfortable they are; they are no longer in their comfort zone.

ACTION PLAN 5

Turn to the action plan in chapter 10. Consider a change that you have recently or will soon be involved with. Perform a 'Force Field Analysis', identifying drivers and restrainers. How did you or how will you remove the restrainers to allow the change to proceed?

Whatever changes you decided to make to your life, or whatever changes are imposed on you at work or home, there will be some discomfort. Not all changes will lead to better conditions. Illness or work changes may lead to a considerable change of lifestyle.

What you need to do is to think through the uncomfortable experience of the change itself and start to plan for the new position; an idea we will return to when looking at positive thinking in the next section.

(In the example at the end of this chapter, Simon is considering a change to the staffing levels at his branches by using more part-time staff in order to improve flexibility.)

The Force Field Analysis technique is one you can use whenever you are faced with a change situation.

POSITIVE THINKING

Positive thinking is a technique that is very useful when dealing with situations of change.

Sue was convinced that she'd never master the new airline booking system. She'd read the manuals and practised. She'd asked advice, but she always seemed to make the same mistake.

'I'll do it right this time, I'll put things in the proper order and make sure that I don't make any mistakes' – but she nearly always did.

In life we tend to fail in those situations we expect to fail in and succeed in those where we expect success. This is connected with the way we talk to ourselves. Lou Tice, who we mentioned earlier, believes that positive 'self talk' is very powerful. We all talk to ourselves, not always aloud, but our thoughts are as much of our communications system as the written word, telephones, etc. They form part of our internal communications system. How many times have you told yourself that 'I can't do this', and found you were right. You have, in fact, created a 'self-fulfilling prophesy'. It is part of a psychological phenomenon called rationalization. If you convince yourself that you can't do something then the failure is mitigated by the fact that at least you had one thing right – you expected to fail and you did; you were right about that.

Sue's mistake is that she was concentrating on the mistakes and not on doing the right thing. If you put the mistakes uppermost in your mind, then the mistakes are what will happen. If you put the 'lure of success' – the doing it right – in your mind, that is what is more likely to happen.

If you tell yourself that 'nobody likes me', don't be surprised if nobody does. Convince yourself that you will pass the examination and you are well on the road to passing it.

Writers on positive thinking and techniques such as neuro-linguistic programming have discovered that 'visualization' is a powerful tool in aiding success. The vast majority of the data we receive and turn into meaningful information is visual; mankind is a visual animal. Our eyes are well developed with stereoscopic and colour vision; even our dreams are visual.

If we can visualize what will happen, our brain, which has difficulty distinguishing fact from fantasy (if this were not true, day-dreams, which are a form of visualization, would not be as pleasant as they are), will begin to believe that this is already reality and our actions will begin to support this 'new' situation.

THINK POINT

Decide on the car you would like to be driving. Be realistic!

Close your eyes and imagine the car being delivered. See the colour, open the door, sit inside. Smell the newness etc.

Spend about a minute putting it into gear and driving off.

It's a nice day, so open the window and sunroof if you've had one fitted.

Do this for a minute each day.

Look at this page a year from now. Are you actually the owner of the car?

Positive self talk and visualization are the two most effective ways to achieve positive thinking.

When running through ideas in your head use the following to ensure that your self talk is positive and not negative:

Be personal: use 'I . . .' – these are your thoughts not anybody else's;

Use present-tense and action verbs: 'I enjoy . . .' ' I gain pleasure out of . . .', 'I am good at . . .'.

By being personal, in the present, and associating actions with, you will begin to convince your brain that this is actually reality. As the brain does not cope well with dissonance, where its perception of reality does not coincide with outside events, subconsciously you will begin to undertake actions that bring you closer to your desired outcome.

Build on the above by spending a short time each day (before rising or in bed at night are often good times), relaxing with a small number of key visualizations. Visualize what you want to happen and put yourself in a situation where it has. Allow yourself to relax and feel good about it. Do not concentrate on how you will achieve it, rather think past this part of the change situation. Do this every day. It takes time but the results can be very enjoyable indeed.

ACTION PLAN 6

In the next action plan (chapter 10), make a list of things you want to achieve within the next year. They can be work goals, material goals, family goals, etc.

Write them down using the ideas above, 'I enjoy . . .', and so forth. Remember they have already happened as far as your brain is concerned. Visualize each one at least once a day.

In a year's time, look back. How many of them have you achieved?

PLANNING

Sue had come to the decision that this was the career that she wanted. She'd enjoyed coming back to work after the children started school, but now she wanted more than a job, she wanted a career. The problem was, however, that she lacked any formal qualifications and she had noticed that her employers were becoming keen on having very well-qualified staff. How could she proceed up the career ladder?

Simon faced a similar dilemma. He gained great satisfaction out of his job and wanted to move on to a regional or headquarters post within three years. The move to Area Manager, however, had cost him his marriage, and he was determined not to repeat the same mistakes of work first and personal life second. How should he chart out his course?

Purists of the positive thinking approach sometimes argue that you've only to keep visualizing something for it to eventually happen. Common sense tells us that we have to be proactive in the process, planning for what we want and considering contingencies for possible changes in direction.

There are three types of situation you need to plan for:

1   Situations where you have a good idea of what might happen. These are everyday situations and both individuals and organizations develop 'Standard Operating Procedures' (SOPs) to deal with them. In the case of the scenario these could include booking standard package holidays and flights. On a personal level they may include planning for a normal family meal or a visit to the shops.
2   There are also those situations that *could well* happen and for which you need some idea of what to do. Your car may break down despite your having planned regular garage visits, so your motoring plans may well include membership of one of the motoring organizations. You may have unexpected guests, so a spare bedroom may be kept ready.
3   There are also situations that hit you like a bolt out of the blue. Careful analysis through your PEST and SWOT may help you spot some of these as they begin to develop, but there will always be the unexpected. Here your plans need to ensure that you are as well prepared mentally and physically as you can be. Keeping your mind and body fit and healthy will assist you in finding the mental and physical energy needed to cope with many of life's unexpected twists and turns.

Sue can look at training courses in order to improve her career prospects and she can plan when to attend. Having two young children, her plans will probably contain contingencies in case they are ill, but only by being in good physical and mental condition could she cope well with something like an unexpected bereavement or the redundancy of her husband.

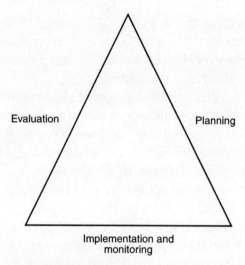

Figure 10 Force Field Analysis

Because the unexpected cannot be planned for in detail, this section will concentrate on planning for what is likely and what may well happen.

Planning forms one side of what may be described as the 'activity triangle' (figure 11).

Planning leads to implementation and monitoring to see that the plan is being followed and that it is leading to the desired outcome. The third side, evaluation, is vital because it is here that you reflect on what happened and use this information to revise future plans. This is how standard operating procedures are developed. Every activity has to have a 'first time', when the plans may be very raw and changed frequently. Through evaluation, it is possible to refine the next 'pass' at the activity so that the plans remain more constant and implementation is smoother.

THINK POINT

Consider the chapter headings in this book. Can you see a link between them and the activity triangle?

The answer should be 'yes':

2 Where am I Now?	Planning
3 Where Do I Want to Get to?	Planning
How am I Going to Get There?	
4 Who is Going With Me?	Planning
What do I Need and Who Can Help?	
5 How Long will it Take?	Planning
6 Am I on the Right Track?	Implementation
How Will I Know When I've Got There?	
7 Where Do I Go from Here?	Evaluation
8 Action Plan	Implementation

Planning is not a linear process, it consists of a series of loops, always checking back to the original objectives. One of the key tasks is to determine what the objectives actually are. This is what you have been doing through your action plan, deciding on what you want to do.

The planning process can be represented schematically in ten steps:

Decide on objectives

Are the objectives in line with personal and work constraints?	(if no, you will need to amend the objectives)
What alternatives will help to achieve the objectives?	
Assess the consequences for each alternative	(if the consequences present major problems, discard or file)

Assess the resources needed for each alternative remaining

Choose the alternative with the least problematic consequences and the least resource implications as your major strategy

Use other remaining alternatives as contingencies

Gather resources

As this takes time, check back to see that your objectives have not changed

Move to implementation phase

You should make a record of each stage, so that you can ensure a logical progression.

Implementation and evaluation are beyond the scope of this section but after implementation and evaluation, you need to ask the key questions:

Did I do what I wanted to do?
Did the plan work?
What changes were made to the plan:
   1) during planning?
   2) during implementation as a result of monitoring?
How would I do it differently next time?

Plans are dynamic. They will, and indeed should, change as circumstances change. When the circumstances change, be prepared to change your plan; carrying on with the original is less likely to lead to success. Changes in plans follow the pattern for all types of change: they are uncomfortable – we deny the need to change the plan, then we defend, then discard, adapt, and finally internalize. The objectives drive the activity, not the plan.

ACTION PLAN 7

Using the action plan in chapter 10, take an activity you need to plan for and use the ten-step planning model introduced above to develop a preferred alternative for implementation.

   After the task is completed, consider whether the plan worked using the ideas in the section.

EXCELLENCE

'Thank John for making the arrangements for that trip the Sales Reps made last week.' Claire had met Helen for a lunchtime chat. 'They said that the service going out and back was superb, although they weren't very happy about the internal flights.'

'I'll ask him to have a word with the airline, they should be good all the time, we're expected to be consistent with all our customers', Helen replied.

'No, it wasn't the same airline. When they came back they were amazed that two flights of about the same length and by coincidence on the same type of plane could be so different. The first plane was slightly better equipped; they had a video and a leg rest and you don't usually expect those in economy, do you.'

'Your firm are so mean, flying them out economy,' Helen interrupted.

'That's not the point, times are hard, but as I was saying, it was the attitude of the people that made the difference. One group were welcoming and nothing was too much trouble, they made plenty of announcements, told the passengers where they were, etc.; it made them feel as though they were important, whatever part of the aircraft they were in. You should know, even economy tickets aren't cheap. The others didn't seem to care. There were no smiles and the service was poor; that's what they really noticed. I'll be writing to John telling him that we'll definitely use the first airline again, but if there's an alternative we'd rather not use the other one.'

The above example is rooted in an actual event. The good airline is not one of the global 'megacarriers', it is the airline of the United Arab Emirates State of Dubai – 'Emirates'. We shall be considering Emirates in further detail in chapter 9, together with two other examples of excellence, chosen from within the travel industry to fit in with the travel agency scenario: namely, British Airways and Princess Cruises (a part of the P&O Group). Chapter 9 is designed to give you a deeper insight into excellence and the 'difference that people make'.

THINK POINT

What organizations do you consider excellent; what is it about the way they operate that leads you to your conclusion?

To what extent is it the physical resources or the human resources that lead you to think that the organization you have chosen is excellent?

The classic work on excellence is *In Search of Excellence* by Tom Peters and Robert Waterman (1982). They looked at a large number of US organizations that had a reputation for excellent products and services, organizations like IBM, Disney, 3M. They found that there were a series of attributes that these companies exhibited: they were all dynamic, they became very customer oriented ('close to the customer'), they gave their people responsibility and backed them when they took risks, they recognized that all productivity comes through people, they made sure that all their employees understood the values and mission of the organization. As organizations they stayed close to what they were good at and didn't try to branch out into unrelated areas, they had simple organization structures, and they kept a close control on values and costs but allowed employees freedom of action within those constraints. Most of those attributes related directly back to the people who worked for (and in these days of partnerships – closely with) the organization.

One thing they postulated was that in excellent organizations, the employees believed that they were the best at whatever the organization did. This is an idea that, perhaps, needs a degree of modification.

A Rolls-Royce is possibly the best car in the world, and in pure terms it is truly excellent. Staff in travel agencies are often asked about the relative merits of similar holidays from different providers. One growing area of business relates to the cruise industry. The most highly rated cruise ship in the world in 1994 (according to the *Berlitz Guide to Cruising and Cruise Ships* (1994)) was Royal Viking Line's *Royal Viking Sun*, but how many people can own a Rolls-Royce or travel on one or two ships? (In 1994, Royal Viking Line operated two vessels.) If the *Royal Viking Sun* and their other vessel, the *Royal Viking Queen*, were full to capacity for 52 weeks of the year, and allowing therefore for 52 seven-day cruises, only 53,000 people would be able to enjoy the experience. No ship will be in operation for 365/6 days without time out for maintenance, and so forth. Rolls-Royce and Royal Viking Line are undeniably excellent – they are probably the best in the world – but for most of us, excellence is connected with things that *we* can do or experience.

Marks and Spencer or Tesco may not be in the same league as very expensive stores, but they offer an excellent service to a large number of customers. Ford Motors may not be perceived as in the same class as Rolls-Royce but they provide good, reliable trans-portation for millions of people across the world. British Airways operates the largest route network in the world and at prices a large number of people can afford, and they do it to a consistent high level of service. Princess Cruise, whom we will discuss later in this chapter, if operating all of their nine vessels (1994) over a full 52-week period on a mixture of 7–21 day cruises could carry approximately 400,000+ passengers in a year. To do that with a consistently high service and at prices that are described as moderate in the Berlitz guide is, for most of us, a truer example of excellence.

Excellence as we would want to present it in this book is a balance between the best service or product for the price with the highest quality, delivered to a consistently high level. All this is done through people. Excellence is the equilibrium between the various components (see figure 12).

If a conscious decision has been made to go for a small 'niche' market, then one cannot compare the products or services so developed with those that are aimed at a wider market. When considering excellence it is important that like is compared with like.

Emirates, British Airways and Princess Cruises all fit this model of excellence: they provide consistent service and quality at a price that makes them accessible to a large number of people and they do it through the attitudes and the competence of their people. You can consider how they achieve this in more detail by reading the appendix, which examines their operations and their people.

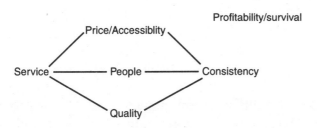

Figure 12 The excellence equilibrium

Service

Sue was on the telephone to a customer who wanted to change a booking. The conversation had begun as so many do: 'I hope you can help me, I've got a problem . . .'

Sue hadn't the experience to deal with the problem, so she called Liz over and explained that the customer had a problem.

'She hasn't any more', Liz replied, 'it's our problem now.'

Remember that you have internal as well as external customers. Everybody you relate to is a customer in the widest sense of the word.

Service is about taking responsibility, going the extra mile. Customers make mistakes, but the essence of good service is when you take responsibility for the problem. You may need to advise them as to what they need to do and there will be things that only they can do (you can't sign forms for them, etc.), but you can show them that they have a 'friend' within the organization. We all have a fair idea of what is acceptable. Excellence is when somebody goes that extra mile, when you do more than they might have expected. If they're angry or upset you may not receive any thanks, but they – and more importantly, you – will know that you did all that you possibly could. There is an important role for the organization here. Unless the organizational competences are present, then the motivation to exercise personal competence will be missing. In the appendix you will read of the faulty shower and the relief steward who took responsibility to have it mended, even though he wasn't an engineer. If he hadn't been trained as to who to see (an organizational competence) he would not have been able to complete the task and end up with a satisfied customer. Smile, even if it is a bad day: it shows that you care.

Consistency

Everybody is entitled to consistency of service or product for the price they have paid. They are entitled to acceptability whatever they have paid. You may not like each of your customers, either internal or external, but if you are concerned about delivering personal excellence, they will all be treated to the same high, consistent standard. People who care about what they do, tend to do it well.

Quality

Quality is never delivering second best. Even if you only have a small part to play in a service or product, play it to your best. Don't cut corners – it only leads to more work. Take pride in what you do. Think about how you can improve what you do. Others will notice, and their performance will improve. Don't tell people how high your standards are (that's a sure way to make enemies): show them by quiet, consistent examples.

Things will go wrong. What do you do to recover the situation?

British Airways ran a training programme for all of their staff worldwide in 1993/4 called 'Winning for Customers'; it focused on those things the ordinary member of the airline could do to assist the customer, and on how to take responsibility and recover when things, as they do, went wrong: when baggage went astray, when connections were lost, when special requirements were needed. Such an organizational competence, needs to be matched by a commitment to personal competence, and only you can make that commitment.

Price/accessibility

You may not control price but you need to understand it. There is a balance between the price somebody is prepared to pay and the price you are prepared to deliver for. Weight it on their side. People are reasonable: they don't want the earth but they do want value for money (or time). British Airways, Tesco, Emirates, Ford, Princess Cruises all deliver value for money. Their service seems better than you would have expected at the price. A British Telecom manager who travelled 40 miles to deliver a fax machine to replace a faulty one in order to save the customer a journey; the person on the street who takes you to a place that is hard to find rather than just give you instructions; all examples of excellence and again all related to people.

A key point about value for money in particular and excellence in general is that talking somebody into something they cannot afford may make you a short-term profit but you are unlikely to see those people again. If you give a value for money product at a price people can afford they will come back. Repeat business is a key organizational performance indicator.

Accessibility is linked to price. As we have stated, like must be compared with like. A lower-priced product or service is likely to be more accessible. Organizations often have two choices: low volume/high margin (Rolls-Royce), or high volume/low margin (Ford). They cater for very different markets and both may be considered excellent in their own way.

ACTION PLAN 8

Think back over the past few weeks. How have you demonstrated excellence? Give examples. On the opposite side of the page in chapter 10, detail improvements you could have made.

SUMMARY

In considering where you want to go, this chapter has looked at your personal plans, how to manage the discomfort of change both by understanding the process, the 'coping cycle' and through techniques such as 'Force Field Analysis' and the ways positive thinking can assist you.

The chapter then considered the planning process and the concept of excellence, a key personal competence.

ACTION PLAN EXAMPLES

(Only a sample set of responses are included in the following.)

4 *Managing change*

Perform a Force Field Analysis on a recent, a current or an anticipated change, identifying drivers and restrainers. Indicate how restrainers were, are being or will be reduced to allow for the change to proceed. In this case Simon is considering the use of replacing full-time staff who leave with more part timers in order to increase flexibility.

Drivers	*Restrainers*
Increased flexibility	More training needed
More staff – greater mix of skills	Part timers are sometimes less committed
Possibility of opening for longer hours	Staffing costs may be higher
	Less career progression

DESIRED DIRECTION OF MOVEMENT ⟶

Reduction of restrainers:

- Consider more cost-effective training programmes
- Ensure that benefit packages assist commitment and motivation
- Increased staff costs will be offset by improved flexibility
- Provide career opportunities for part-time staff

6 *Positive thinking*

Make a list of things you want to achieve within the next year. They can be work goals, material goals, family goals, etc.

Write them down using the ideas above: 'I enjoy ...', etc. Remember they have already happened as far as your brain is concerned. Visualize each one at least once a day.

In a year's time, look back. How many of them have you achieved? (The following example is for Helen.)

- New car (I enjoy driving my Vauxhall Astra to work each day.)

- Complete training programme (It gave me great pleasure completing stage 1 of the company's training programme.)
- Achieve opportunities for travel (I am pleased that my work gives me the opportunity to travel to interesting places.)

7 Planning

Take an activity you need to plan for and use the ten-step planning model introduced above to develop a preferred alternative for implementation.

After the task is completed, consider whether the plan worked using the ideas in the section. (The following is for Sue's family holiday.)

DECIDE ON OBJECTIVES   *write them down*

Family holiday with relaxation for Mum and Dad and plenty of activities for the children, within the agreed budget. Preferably in August for the school holidays. Children would like to visit Disneyland.

ARE THE OBJECTIVES IN LINE   *if no, you will need to amend*
WITH PERSONAL AND WORK   *the objectives*
CONSTRAINTS?

Yes, holiday rota shows that there will be the opportunity for 2 weeks in August at both our firms. Budget agreed.

WHAT ALTERNATIVES WILL HELP
TO ACHIEVE THE OBJECTIVES?

Disneyland (California)
Disneyland (Florida)
EuroDisney
American Family Cruises

ASSESS THE CONSEQUENCES FOR   *if the consequences present*
EACH ALTERNATIVE   *major problems, discard or file*

Disneyland California   Long flight, over budget

Disneyland Florida	Plenty of other attractions, within budget
EuroDisney	Weather may be bad. Children would prefer USA
American Family Cruises	Good activities but designed for American families

ASSESS THE RESOURCES NEEDED FOR EACH ALTERNATIVE REMAINING

Disneyland California	£XXXX
Disneyland Florida	£YYYY
EuroDisney	£ZZZZ + family car to go as well
American Family Cruises	£AAAA

CHOOSE THE ALTERNATIVE WITH THE LEAST PROBLEMATIC CONSEQUENCES AND THE LEAST RESOURCE IMPLICATIONS AS YOUR MAJOR STRATEGY

Disneyland Florida

USE OTHER REMAINING ALTERNATIVES AS CONTINGENCIES

EuroDisney (others too expensive)

| GATHER RESOURCES | record them as they are in place |

Complete this section as necessary

AS THIS TAKES TIME, CHECK BACK TO SEE THAT YOUR OBJECTIVES HAVE NOT CHANGED

No they haven't

MOVE TO IMPLEMENTATION PHASE

At the end of the task ask yourself: (they went to Florida and had a great time):

DID I DO WHAT I WANTED TO DO?

Yes

DID THE PLAN WORK?

Yes

WHAT CHANGES WERE MADE TO PLAN:

1) during planning?

Changed to end of July because of vacancies at the resort.

2) during implementation as a result of monitoring?

Hired a car. We didn't think we'd need one but we wanted to see other things as well

HOW WOULD I DO IT DIFFERENTLY NEXT TIME?

Check other attractions and the need for a car before departure

8 Excellence

(For Helen)

Think back over the past few weeks. How have you demonstrated excellence? Give examples. On the opposite side of the sheet detail improvements you could have made.

a) *Service*	*Improvements*
Changed booking for Mr Y	Don't let customer know that this was causing so much extra work
b) *Consistency*	
Monitored time taken to make bookings	Found I was giving slightly quicker attention to more expensive bookings
c) *Quality*	
Checked ticket packs going to customers	Ensure all are neat and tidy
d) *Value for money*	
Found good holiday for large family at budget rates	Remember about repeat business

4

Who is Going With Me, What do I Need and Who Can Help?

From the moment she got up this morning Liz had known it was going to be one of those days. She had overslept and had been rushing ever since. Not that she was late for work; but she was later than she had planned to be. By now she should have cleared that outstanding report for Simon that she hadn't had time to finish last night. Instead everyone else would be arriving in five minutes and the phone would start ringing; she would never get it done now and would probably have to stay late again tonight.

That would mean another row with Alan. He would be home at about two o'clock because there wasn't much work available in his line of business at the moment. He would start to brood as the afternoon wore on, and by the time she rang him to say she was staying late he would be ready to go off the deep end.

Why couldn't he realize that it wasn't her fault that she had to stay late? She was only doing it for both their benefits anyway. As his job wasn't bringing in all that much it was important that she did well at hers. Couldn't he see that?

She could hear him now: 'Not again! You promised to be home on time today. I've arranged to meet Brenda and Justin at the pub; as we agreed, remember?'

She would say, 'Look, I have to show willing. Simon expects it. One of us has to earn some money!'

The phone would go dead like it did the last time. She knew that she had gone too far last time, giving the impression that Alan's job was far less important than hers. Still, they had enjoyed making it up!

Oh well, never mind, it might not come to that if she could get a bit of space to herself during the day to complete the report.

The telephone rang. It was Jason. He wouldn't be able to come in today as he had a migraine. She made the usual noises of sympathy that were required in such situations, but she felt a wave of resentment at the fact that he hadn't been able to make the effort to come in. She was mentally working out how to cover his job for the day when Sue arrived.

'That's okay, I'll look after it. I don't need to rush home today because Tony gets home at three o'clock and he's going to watch the live international match on the TV. I might as well work late here.'

'What, a football match, on TV today?'

'Yes, didn't you hear Jason going on about it yesterday?'

'No wonder he's got a migraine today then, very convenient!'

John had arrived. As he hung his coat up, he glanced over to Liz. 'Simon's coming at ten o'clock, did you know?'

'No, what for?' Liz replied.

'I thought you might be able to tell me, as he seems to keep you in the picture more than me.'

'He only tells me when you're not here.'

'Whatever. At least make sure that everyone knows that he's coming so that they can be on their guard. We don't want to give him any ammunition do we?'

Well, thought Liz. We could do with a few changes around here. All John wants is a quiet life. At least Simon makes things happen. He tells you what he wants and you know exactly where you stand with him. Which is more than can be said for John; he was so bitter, you could never tell what he was up to.

'Yes, okay, I'll make sure everyone knows and that everything is done properly.'

'Yes, I'm sure you will', mumbled John, and went into his office.

At that point Sue hurriedly followed John into his office. 'Actually', she said quietly, 'I know why he's coming. I took the message from his secretary. He wants to talk to you about a new firm that has just moved into the area. He thinks there may be possibilities. I assumed you knew.'

'Okay, thanks Sue, forget about it. But don't mention this to anyone else yet. I'll let Liz know if anything comes of it.'

Typical, thought John. He has to stick his oar into everything. Well, if it's that large engineering firm that opens up officially next week, he had played golf with the MD last Thursday and had arranged a formal meeting with him next week. That would show Simon. In the meantime, Liz could sweat about what it was about.

John knew that she was worried about a report that she had to complete for him. Well, let her worry whether it was that! It would do her good!

He sat down and started to look through his in tray. He didn't trust Simon. And he didn't trust Liz! Thank heavens he could rely on Sue, she was pretty straight.

Well, the day is only a few minutes old and attitudes have already been well and truly struck!

Liz has made assumptions about Simon, John, Jason and her husband Alan.

John has made assumptions about Simon and Liz, and also about Sue.

The potential for conflict appears to be great!

THINK POINT

Now, consider the facts of the situation. Let's leave the attitudes to one side for the moment.

The facts:

Liz has arrived at work a little later than she wanted to but is still in good time for work.

Liz has a heavy workload and *may* have to stay late at work to finish the report.

Jason has rung in to say that he is ill.

Sue is prepared to cover Jason's work for the day.

Simon is arriving at ten o'clock to discuss a business opportunity with John.

Sue had not told John what the meeting with Simon was about because she thought he already knew. She has now corrected this.

How much potential for conflict is there in the bare facts themselves?

Well, Liz has a heavy workload and may have to stay late, while Sue has covered the problem of Jason not coming to work. The problem does not really lie in what is actually going on but on the attitudes that people have towards each other. The problem is rather one of Perception.

One of the most common phenomena is the Halo/Horns effect. Someone performs a task well and we assume that he or she will perform other tasks well. This is the Halo effect.

Someone wears a sloppy uniform while representing her organization and we assume that everyone in that organization is sloppy: the Horns effect.

This is one of the reasons why it is imperative that staff who meet customers should be smart, helpful and carry out the job well. A customer's idea of an airline is likely to be set by the first representative that they meet, for example, check-in staff. A bad impression created here will make it difficult for the cabin crew to appear in a good light.

A head waiter who welcomes you to a restaurant will set the tone for the evening. Those who see the Halo will welcome the chef's recommendation. Those who see the Horns will mutter about leftovers from lunchtime.

Let's go back to the agency.

John certainly views Simon and Liz with Horns. Everything they do is suspicious. At the same time he has forgiven Sue for her lapse in not telling him what the meeting was about because he is still seeing the Halo of her previous behaviour. Meanwhile, Liz thinks the worst of Jason.

Clearly, we all perceive things in different ways. You only need to take a lover of classical music into a record shop with loud disco music playing to realize that they are not reacting to it in the same way as you are!

We often assume that because we perceive something in a certain way, then others will see it in the same way too.

Supporters of opposing sides in a game of football may well see completely different versions of the same match, because they are looking at it from different perspectives. It's rather odd that fouls or hand balls, leading to penalty kicks are usually only seen by one set of supporters!

We also see ourselves in a different way from that in which others see us.

Luft and Ingham (1955) developed a framework to demonstrate this. It is called the Johari Window. The window consists of four areas:

- The open area which is that part of ourselves that is both known to us and revealed to other people.
- The hidden area contains those things we know about ourselves but are not prepared to divulge to other people.
- The blind area covers those things that people are aware of in us but of which we are not aware ourselves.
- The unknown area is one that is neither known to ourselves or revealed to other people but which influences our behaviour.

When we first meet other people we may well disclose very little of ourselves and the open area may be relatively small. As we get to know people better we are likely to let more and more of ourselves, our beliefs and attitudes become known. The open area thus becomes larger and the hidden area smaller.

In order to increase the open area further it is necessary to reduce the blind area. This can be done by seeking and accepting feedback from other people.

As the open area grows and the hidden and blind areas reduce it is very likely that there will be some reduction of the unknown area, and that may lead to greater and greater self-awareness.

In the agency John may well have a relatively small open area at the moment. He keeps things close to his chest and does not invite feedback from his staff. He seems to fear feedback from Simon!

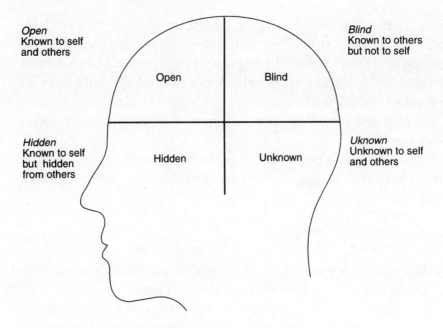

Figure 13 Johari's Window
Source: adapted from Luft and Ingham,

THINK POINT

Consider the Johari Window. How can you start to increase your own self-awareness? What will be your first step?

At ten o'clock Simon arrived and went into John's office. Simon wanted to explore ways of gaining new business from the firms that were moving into the nearby trading estate and wanted to discuss a marketing exercise with John. The meeting went on until lunchtime, when both of them emerged. Simon went over to Liz, 'Could you join us for lunch, we're just going down to the pub for a quick bite?'

'Oh, I'm pretty tied up, I've got that report to . . .'

'Oh, there's no rush for that at the moment, the end of next week will do.'

A weight visibly lifted from Liz's shoulders; she had thought that he wanted it immediately. She wouldn't have to stay late after all. 'Well, in that case, thank you, I'll get my coat.'

They went out and that left only Sue and Helen in the office. 'Typical', said Helen, 'I'd arranged to meet Claire for lunch, now I won't be able to make it; I can't go out leaving you to hold the fort on your own. I'd better ring her.'

'Yes, it was rather inconsiderate, but I don't expect they'll be long. Why don't you see if she can meet you a little later and you can go when they come back. I'm sure Liz won't be long; she has lots of work to do.'

It was three o'clock when they all returned. Helen had put Claire off a second time. She was a bit upset and told Liz so.

'She's not just a friend of mine, she puts a lot of business our way. She wasn't very impressed, I can tell you.'

Liz considered for a moment. Yes, she had been inconsiderate. She had wanted to go along with Simon and John because she thought there might have been some advantage for her and didn't want to miss anything. As it turned out, it had been rather boring and in the meantime she had shown lack of consideration for one of her staff and shown the company in a bad light to a customer.

THINK POINT

Consider the last time you were inconsiderate to a member of your staff. How could you have avoided it? What can you do in the future to avoid it happening again?

'I'm sorry Helen, I just didn't think. You can have first lunch tomorrow.'

Helen rang Claire and arranged to see her the next day.

Later that afternoon, Jason's mother rang to say that she had had to call the doctor out and he had sent Jason to hospital for some tests. The family was quite worried about him.

Closing time arrived and the team had survived another day. However, let's look back at some of the tensions that existed earlier in the day:

Jason was apparently quite ill and Liz had been wrong to doubt him.

Simon's visit was quite routine. John had even enjoyed it as it gave him a new challenge. Simon had been quite supportive and had asked John to let him know if he required any additional resources.

Liz did not have to work late and so any potential conflict with Alan was avoided . . . at least for today.

Let's have a look at conflict in a little more detail.

For every person there are a number of different pressures pulling him or her in different directions. The model in figure 14 illustrates this:

You have your own development needs which point you in one direction. At the same time there are pressures within your job that prevent you from achieving this. People studying for qualifications while doing their normal full job of work are continually torn between meeting their work objectives and studying.

At the same time, people at work, or outside, may expect different things from you. Colleagues may want you to join them in the evening for a drink. Or your boss may expect you to work overtime every day.

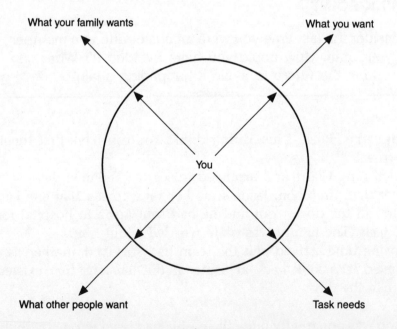

Figure 14 Different pressures pull in different directions

Your family, too, is very important, and they may be pulling you in another direction still. They may not want you to work the overtime or to join your colleagues for a drink, or study for your qualification. They may simply want to spend some time with you.

The end result is that you are continually being pulled in different directions. One of the major problems here, however, is that the more you are pulled in one direction the more you resent being pulled in that direction, and eventually conflict occurs.

Different people will have different responses to these pressures according to the type of person they are. People who feel that their family is very important and the needs of others less important are likely to allow family pressures to pull them some way before conflict ensues. On the other hand, they may quickly resent the pressure put on them by other people.

Figure 15 shows how this conflict might be managed.

Here, all of the pressures are pulling in roughly the same direction. At the moment, John is a fairly good example of this. He finds it difficult to grow in the current situation, but he does want to develop into the job because he wants to continue to

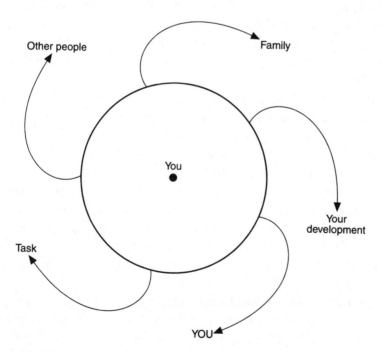

Figure 15 Managing the conflicting pressures

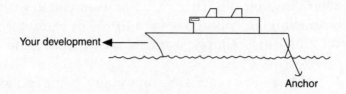

Your development ◄—

Anchor

Figure 16 Individual and family pulling apart

provide for his family. His wife, Eileen, has no job at the moment and can look after things at home if he needs to put in a bit of extra work. To his surprise, Simon has been very supportive this morning. He has agreed some very clear objectives with him which are mutually acceptable. At the same time he wants some of his former status and self-esteem back, and success in this project will go a long way towards this.

There are people who want to help him too, as we will see a little later.

So John, though he may not realize it yet, is in a strong position to move forward.

For anyone who is looking to develop themselves it is unlikely that they will able to do so successfully if they alienate their family. The family can be an immense support in times of stress, and will be a cause of stress itself if conflict arises. Figures 16, 17 and 18 illustrate this point.

Here, the person who is trying to manage their own development sees the family as an anchor, which is a dead weight, the force of which has to be removed or in some way overcome before progress can be made. The movement from the support of the family is outwards and eventually something will have to give, either the family or the development. In such cases development may cease or the family may tear itself apart.

On the other hand, in figure 17 the family is also seen as an anchor, but one that is there for support and which can help the person keep their feet on the ground while they are developing.

The movement is gradually outward in a spiral as the person grows, always remaining near the values and support provided by the family. In this case it is likely that the family will grow with the person being developed.

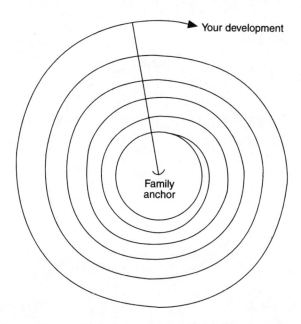

Figure 17 Family providing support and pulling together

THINK POINT

What is Liz's situation here? Clearly, she is on the ship headed out to sea! So how can we avoid this?

Continuing the maritime theme, we can use the seven Cs strategy (figure 18). Let's look at this strategy in respect of Liz.

Has she really shown *consideration* for Alan? Her own job is going very well at the moment, rather exciting with some excellent opportunities. Alan, on the other hand, is going through a bad patch and himself needs consideration and support. Liz has not really looked at things from his point of view.

In what way is she *co-operating* with Alan? She spends time studying. She works late on occasions in order to impress the boss. Alan spends long periods on his own brooding about his current lack of success. It might be possible, for example, for Alan to study for a qualification or skill which may help him to develop, at the same time as Liz. Or she could set out periods in which she would neither study nor work.

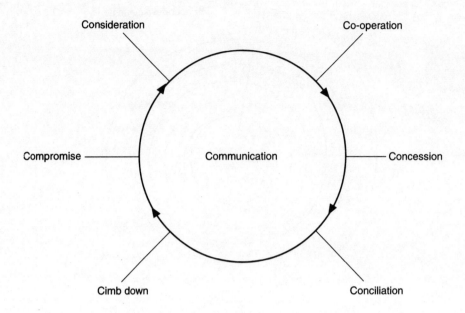

Figure 18 The seven Cs strategy

There may well have to be a *compromise* somewhere. Perhaps Alan could look for ways in which he might expand the business during his slack time. He might also look to do the household administration so that when Liz is free they can spend some quality time together.

Concessions may need to be given by both parties. Liz may have to lower her ambitions while Alan may have to consider whether there might be opportunities for him in other parts of the country.

Earlier, Liz was quite angry at what Alan might say, even though she hadn't spoken to him at the time and neither she nor he was aware at that time whether there was actually going to be a problem. She automatically assumed that her job was the most important, even though her success was relatively new and Alan's lack of it was too. She needs to *climb down* from this rather lofty position and talk to Alan on equal terms.

Almost any conflict can be resolved if there is a genuine desire for *conciliation*. People have to want to make the effort. They must see the resolution of the conflict as being highly desirable and subordinate their own particular interests to it.

Finally, *communication*, as ever, is the important link. The most important aspects are

- listening to what is actually meant rather than to what is being said;
- being perceptive to the other person's body language;
- looking at the situation from the other person's point of view. How would *you* feel in the same position?

THINK POINT

Consider a recent conflict that you had either at home or at work. How might the seven Cs have helped to resolve the matter more quickly?

Helen met Claire for lunch the next day. It turned out to be an interesting meeting. Helen had been talking to Claire last week about her dissatisfaction with the way her job was going. She wasn't really sure whether this was the right job for her. There wasn't really anything for her to get her teeth into.

She had told Claire about Simon's visit yesterday and about the new campaign, which she thought might be interesting, but didn't really involve her.

'Well, why not get involved?' suggested Claire.

'What do you mean, get involved?'

'Why don't you speak to John and ask him if you can help with the campaign? It would give you something interesting to do. You never know, John may be wondering how he is going to manage it on his own. He may feel unwilling to ask for help because he knows that it is his responsibility and everyone else is so busy at the moment.'

'Well, yes we are busy, but I'm sure that I could spare some time if it was going to prove useful. The only thing is . . . I'm not sure that I can help. I've never been involved in that sort of thing before. What could I do?'

'I could tell you what our department needs from a travel agency and that might give you a few ideas that you could suggest to John. He might invite you to help him.'

'Brilliant idea.'

'Well, we like to deal with someone we can trust and rely on to get things right. We don't want people ending up in Paris when they're supposed to be in Amsterdam!

We like a good discount, which goes without saying of course!

We like things to be made easy for us. Things like:

- getting through first time on the phone
- urgent mail being sent to us first by first-class post or even by hand
- polite staff to deal with, just like you!
- a whole range of products on sale, from airline tickets and first-class hotels to package holidays for the staff outing
- an agency that is prepared to arrange the difficult itineraries – anyone can do the simple ones. One that we trust to work out and arrange these complicated bookings goes a long way to giving customer satisfaction in our book.'

'Thanks Claire, but that's pretty obvious stuff. Surely John will be aware of all that, it's his job after all.'

'Well, yes, but this is straight from the customer, a piece of primary market research. I doubt if you've got anything as explicit as that from many customers. Why not design a market research questionnaire and suggest to John that you interview some of the companies involved. I'll be your first interviewee!'

'Yes, that could work. If John likes the idea, then he may ask me to get involved, and that could be really interesting. I'll try it. Thanks Claire, the meal's on me today.'

Helen returned to the office in high spirits and after a quick coffee she knocked on John's door.

ACTION PLAN 9

Helen is taking a positive, assertive attitude here. She is not going to wait for someone to ask her. She is going to try to get involved. Think of some project going on at work that you would like to be involved in. What steps can you take so that the person in charge will take notice of your interest?

Identify what particularly interests you

You may find that there is some area of work outside the scope of your present job that you feel would be useful for your development. It may be possible for you to take it on in addition to your current duties. For example, people who are working towards Management qualifications often have to carry out a work-based project as part of their studies.

Decide who can help you

It may be possible to approach the person who controls the area in which you are interested who may not be your own boss. They may be happy to have a volunteer to help them. On the other hand, it may be best to approach your own boss, who may be their colleague and therefore have more influence.

Try to enlist their help

In both cases you need to be aware that not everyone is comfortable when people volunteer to do things. Your boss may feel that if you have some spare time you should do more for them. Or other people in the department in which the work is based may feel jealous at the apparently preferential treatment which you are being given. Considerable tact may be needed and you may have to learn to cope with rejection.
  Now turn to chapter 10 and fill in your Action Plan.

John's first reaction was defensive.
  'I didn't ask anyone for any ideas. I've only just agreed the objectives myself, I haven't had time to think about it yet. Give me time to think and let you know if I want any help.'
  Helen left the office dejected.
  Sue, who had just made coffee and had overheard the whole thing through John's open door, smiled at Helen and went into the office with John's coffee.

'You were a little hard on her, you know, she was only trying to help. Now you've put the barriers up and she's totally demotivated.'

'Well, these young people today, they don't give you any time to get your ideas together. They rush in as if we were incapable of thinking of any. I'll show them I can do this, you just watch.'

'I know you can do it. But Helen doesn't know that *she* can do it. This is an opportunity for her to express herself and to see what she can do. She's looking to you to give her a chance to show what she can do to help. She's not competing; she's trying to help *you* achieve.'

John thought for a moment. He had a lot of respect for Sue's opinion. So why shouldn't he respect Helen's opinion too? He had to admit that he was far too quick to find insults where none were intended. He had to give people a chance.

The blind spot in John's Johari Window has just opened a little bit further, thanks to Sue's feedback!

THINK POINT

Have you ever treated suggestions as threats? John clearly had not listened to Helen properly, nor had he read her body language. He needs to get to know his staff better. Consider the steps you intend to take to ensure that you don't make the same mistake.

John asked Helen to come back into the office and apologised. He then told her that he welcomed her suggestions and looked forward to working with her.

THINK POINT

How many of the seven Cs has John used here?

Clearly he has begun to *listen*, so he has started to *communicate*. He has *climbed down* from his entrenched position and has sought *conciliation* with Helen. He has also begun to treat her with more *consideration*. Now they can look forward to *co-operating* on the new business venture.

John and Helen sat down and discussed her questionnaire and other suggestions for a marketing campaign to win over the new businesses in the area. At the end of the session both felt exhilarated. They had set out a plan, agreed objectives that each of them needed to meet, and deadlines by which each objective should be completed. They had made a list of resources that they needed from head office, and John had agreed to take Simon up on his offer here. The most vital thing would be some secretarial support, as there was not sufficient spare capacity within the branch to encompass the extra work. The other important aspect was money. John and Helen had made an estimate of how much the extra materials for the campaign would cost, and had drawn up a budget which they needed Simon to sanction from head office.

In the event, Simon was as good as his word and readily agreed to give them all the support they needed.

The final element of support that was needed from Simon was to agree to some additional training for Helen to enable her to be more effective in the campaign.

Both Helen and John went home in excellent spirits that evening.

The next day John gave some thought about the best method of developing Helen's knowledge of the business market. He wondered what sort of person she was and what method would be the most effective for her.

In *In Charge, Managing People* you were introduced to the Kolb Learning Cycle, and the ways in which different people prefer to learn as set out by Peter Honey and Alan Mumford in their *Manual of Learning Styles* (1986).

Kolb identified four steps in the learning cycle:

1 Experiencing – actually doing something
2 Evaluating – analysing what happened
3 Conceptualizing – thinking about why things happen
4 Experimenting – turning new ideas to practical use

Honey and Mumford suggested that different people prefer to enter the learning cycle at different stages. He identified four different types to correspond with the four stages:

1   Activists prefer to experience. They learn best when they can get their teeth into a new situation that they have not met before and enjoy solving the problems they encounter.

   They learn least when they have to take a passive role while someone tells them what they should be doing.

2   Reflectors prefer to evaluate. They learn best from evaluating what has happened. They need plenty of time for reflection in order to analyse fully all the implications.

   They learn least from being asked to carry out one activity, and then to move on quickly to another without having sufficient time to think about and fully assimilate what has happened so far.

3   Theorists prefer to conceptualize. They learn best from considering the theory of how something might work. They want to know what is likely to happen and why, and prefer to have such details before they try anything. They can then fit what actually happens into this theoretical framework. They also like to be able to fit the task they are doing into the overall task so that they can see how their actions affect others.

   They learn least when they have to try something without having the opportunity to consider the theoretical implications first.

4   Pragmatists prefer to experiment. They like to try out new ideas in practice to see how they work. They are practical people who can see the link between the theory and the practice. They are likely to experiment in a smaller area to see if the theory works before attempting it in a wider situation.

   They learn least when there is no immediate opportunity to put the theory into a practical situation.

THINK POINT

What sort of person do you think Helen is? Which do you think would be most suitable learning style for her? Would John prefer the same style?

Helen is likely to be a pragmatist. She likes to try out new ideas to see if they work. If John leaves her to develop the market research questionnaire she will try it out on a limited number of people and if it works she will immediately apply it to the marketing campaign. If she were asked to develop it with no immediate intention of putting it to some use she would soon lose interest.

John too has a learning curve to undertake. His knowledge of the business travel market is rather sketchy at best. He is likely to be a reflector. He will want to evaluate results at every stage before moving on to the next. He is unlikely to be at his best if he has to deal with a number of activities in quick succession before he has time to work out the implications of the first one.

John and Helen are likely to make a good team here. The situation probably does not call for an activist, who will dive in before fully considering all of the implications. Any of the other three styles would probably be best, and the team of John and Helen has two of those styles.

THINK POINT

What sort of learning style do you think suits you best?

Tom Peters, in his book *Thriving on Chaos* (1987, p. 261), places particular emphasis on learning from failure. He calls it 'failing forward'. He argues that mistakes are a really excellent thing for an organization to make because the more they make the more they learn from them. Conversely, organizations that don't make any are unlikely to be innovative enough for today's marketplace.

Indeed, he argues that rather than conceptualize about products to try to get them absolutely right, organizations should try them out in the field. He calls it a 'do a pilot' mentality rather than 'write a proposal' mentality (1987, p. 207).

This fits in with the earlier work of Peters and Waterman, *In Search of Excellence*, where they talk about organizations having 'a bias for action'. This is covered in more detail in *In Charge, Managing Operations*.

This would seem to suggest that Activists might be rather important in organizations today. Perhaps John and Helen should enlist the help of Simon rather more than just in a resource-providing role.

It is certainly true that the pace of change in the environment is so fast now that organizations which cannot bring their ideas to the market-place quickly are likely to lose out to the competition.

So what does 'fail forward' offer us in our travel agency.

Well, both John and Helen are relatively inexperienced in the business area. However, they are both feeling motivated to find a solution, and may well bring new solutions that haven't been considered before because of their fresh approach. They are very likely to make some errors along the way, but as long as they learn from them quickly and make the necessary adjustments it is likely to leave them and the company stronger in the long run.

ACTION PLAN 10

Think of two new ideas that would be worth trying out in your own organization. Turn to chapter 10 and make an entry in your Action Plan.

John and Helen are both looking forward to the new challenge, and they are adopting a 'Can Do' approach. This is very important. Often in organizations this can be a cultural issue. When you interact with them you can usually tell straight away whether they are Can Do or Can't Do. Let's look at some examples.

You are trying to ensure a delivery for your client tomorrow morning. 'I don't suppose it would be possible for you to deliver that tomorrow, I know it's a bit short notice,' said with a grimace on your face, is likely to invite the answer 'No it's not.'

A bright and cheerful 'My client would like it to be delivered tomorrow if possible' may well bring a 'Yes'. Similarly, 'I know this is going to be difficult and you probably can't manage it' will be met with 'You're right it is and we can't!'

You can be sure that if John and Helen were to adopt a 'Can't Do' approach they would soon, indeed, find that it could not be done!

In a Can Do approach you will find that all of the following are involved:

Thought – you feel and think that of course you can do it
Action – you take the necessary action to ensure it happens
Manner of communication – polite, bright and assertive
Body language – smile, look interested, nod in anticipation of agreement

---

THINK POINT

Be truthful with yourself. Have you ever adopted a 'Can't Do' attitude at the beginning of a task? What was the result?

ACTION PLAN 11

Now turn to your action plan in chapter 10 and list down the next two tasks that you are going to do. Identify how you are going to ensure that you adopt a 'Can Do' approach.

Over the last couple of days we have seen a number of the staff in the agency interacting with each other. We have seen some of them at their best and others at their worst. Let's look now at one of the major factors present today which can affect all of us: that is, stress.

We have all found ourselves suffering from stress. It is not just the high-powered executive who suffers from it. Primitive tribes too have pressures on their simple life-style which take their toll in the form of stress.

Stress can be very debilitating, and in its more extreme forms can be truly devastating.

In the USA, T. H. Holmes and R. J. Rahe (1967) produced a 'social readjustment rating scale' in which various life events were rated according to the amount of stress they produce. The scale is not reproduced here, nor is there any attempt to give any of the following causes any kind of rating. Many of the causes rated by Holmes and Rahe are included in the following lists.

Let's now look at some of the causes of stress. We can group them into home related and work related.

Home related:
Bereavement
Attending a funeral
Divorce or separation
Illness or injury
Getting married
Becoming pregnant
Giving birth
Sexual problems
Other marital problems
Causing or being involved in an accident
Financial worries
Buying a house
Moving house
Going on holiday
Major purchases, e.g. a car
Forced change of life-style
Putting on weight
Dieting
Christmas
Committing an offence
Children's behaviour
Retirement
Wife/husband changing/leaving job
Noisy or troublesome neighbours

Work related:
Being dismissed or giving in your resignation
Losing status
Financial problems at work, especially self-employed
Changing jobs
Problems with your boss or higher management
Changing hours of work
Commuting to and from work
Lack of control in your own job
Behaviour of colleagues
Having or causing an accident at work
Feeling responsible for something major going wrong at work
Failure to meet objectives, especially missing deadlines.

Now let's look at some of these in more detail:

Home related

There are no easy answers here. Often, professional counselling is needed. The main point here is to recognize that you or anyone in your team is likely to feel some kind of stress if even one of these factors is present. For many people several of them might apply all at once. Not everyone will need professional help, but they will all need understanding and support from their boss and their colleagues.

Support may be offered in several ways, ranging from allowing time off for serious matters such as bereavement to:

visiting colleagues who are in hospital or who are all ill at home
offering a kindly word
provide a friendly ear so that people can get the problem off their chest
giving advice where it is wanted
helping financially if it is warranted or possible
putting people in touch with others who may have undergone a similar experience and who may be able to help them through the problem

not saying anything when someone clearly does not want to
talk about it

being there when needed.

If it is yourself who is affected then it may help if you have
colleagues who can help you in some of the ways mentioned
above. Remember, you are bound to have a different perspective
on the problem, and you may need to make allowances for people
who are genuinely trying to help but only succeed in making you
feel worse.

Work related

Again the key word here is *support*. However, it is likely that in a
work situation you can offer a lot more than psychological or
friendly support. You may be able to change things and therefore
reduce the stress felt by the members of your team. Or your boss
or your colleagues (together with you) may be able to alter factors
that are causing you stress. You may be able to change some of
them yourself!

Let's look at things you can tackle yourself:

- commuting
- changing jobs
- changing hours
- leaving work

Do you really want to commute to and from work? Are there
alternatives? Could you move house to be nearer work, or move
jobs to be nearer home? Do you really want to work the new
hours?

You need to consider how much you enjoy your current job and
what you will gain by changing it; for example, more responsibility, a more challenging and interesting job, easier home circumstances. Often we seek promotion to a job which offers a little bit
more money but which is not really what we enjoy doing. Is this
trade-off worth it?

With respect to leaving work, in cases of dismissal, you need to
carry out the disciplinary procedures correctly and fairly and

treat the member of staff with respect, even though you no longer want him or her to work for you. Similarly, hitting the managing director after he or she has fired you may give you an immediate surge of satisfaction, but it will cause you some angst in the long run. Remember, it may still be possible to stay friends with some of your former colleagues and you may be grateful for their support.

The same applies if you resign to move on to pastures new. There is more to be gained by leaving in a friendly atmosphere than in parting in acrimony. There are numerous examples of people who have left a firm in the latter circumstances only to find that the person whom they insulted on their last day was a major customer of the new company who they are going to work for, and in a position to put a lot of work their way (or not!).

In today's high-tech world more and more work is carried out by fewer and fewer people. In addition, the very competitive environment that most organizations face leads them to try to reduce costs as much as they can. In many, staff costs account for a high proportion of the total costs (often as much as 70 per cent). This has led to a large amount of pressure on jobs and many organizations have reduced the number of staff they employ. Even industries where jobs were considered to be for life or at least very secure have not been spared.

The result of this is that people generally are very much more concerned about their job security. Many can be said to have slipped down Maslow's 'hierarchy of needs' which we met in *In Charge, Managing People*.

Not only does redundancy affect the people who lose their jobs, but the entire family too. Indeed, John's wife, Eileen, has recently been made redundant and this has caused additional stress on John, not only from the financial point of view, but also from the need to bolster her self esteem.

So if you find yourself worrying about the future, what can you do?

Well, certainly it would be useful to develop your personal competences. In the current climate job security may best be expressed in terms of the marketable skills that people possess. The more skills they have, the less likely they are to find themselves out of a job. And if they do, then the more likely it is that they will find themselves a new one.

This move away from a job for life approach brings not only threats for potential employees. It may also bring opportunities. Those with a high level of skills may well find themselves in demand from several employers and may well be able to negotiate a favourable deal. Others may work for several employers on a subcontract basis, concentrating in each case on doing work in which they are really interested.

So if you find yourself in this situation, remember there are steps that you personally can take to increase your own opportunities.

Now let's look at problems that require other people to help.

Problems with your boss or colleagues may well be possible to solve by using the seven Cs strategy mentioned earlier in this chapter. Remember to treat other people the way you would like to be treated!

Lack of control in your job can be very stressful, especially if your boss has no idea how much pressure you are under. He may load extra work onto you, or perhaps even worse: waste your time by keeping you sitting in his office while he talks on the phone about his holiday; or make you attend a meeting when there is no real need to do so. Especially when you are trying to meet a deadline!

It is perhaps necessary to examine the difference between pressure and stress.

Pressure is likely to spur us on to achieve, and might involve setting difficult but achievable targets within tight, but achievable time-scales. Pressure can be very motivating. Many people say that they work best when under pressure and indeed, may find it difficult to achieve anything without it.

We could describe pressure as being a *constructive* force.

Stress, on the other hand, is likely to involve unachievable work-loads or deadlines and is rarely motivating.

We could describe stress as a *destructive* force.

This brings us to missing deadlines as a cause of stress. Here we can also include failure in general, including causing financial problems or accidents at work. The main point to make here is the one that Tom Peters makes: that is, to *learn* from the experience and make adjustments so that it does not happen again.

Well, there are some of the causes of stress, but how do we recognize it both in ourselves and in others?

RECOGNIZING STRESS

Let's look at some of the symptoms:

tiredness, either through overwork or lack of sleep
irritability
rapid mood swings
making silly errors
fidgeting
staring into space with a taut, glazed expression
displaced activity (e.g. throwing yourself into spring
   cleaning)
eating/drinking/smoking more than usual
taking time off work
withdrawing from interaction with colleagues or family

You can probably list many others!

In order to deal with stress you first have to realize and accept that you are suffering from it! Once you have recognized this you can look at the causes of stress outlined above to see if you can eliminate it. While you are working out a strategy for eliminating the cause of stress there are several coping techniques that you can use to help.

- Spend time on a hobby such as reading or riding or other physical exercise such as swimming. This helps your mind to focus on other things (or on nothing) and may help you to set the problem into perspective.
- Try exercises involving flexing and relaxing the muscles in your body, usually in conjunction with breathing exercises. Certainly, slowing your breathing down has a very calming effect. Try taking some slow deep breaths before your next important meeting. You might be surprised how much it helps.
- Avoid caffeine in coffee and tea. This has the effect of stimulating you, but the effect does not last long, and in some people can lead to a feeling of depression once the caffeine wears off.
- Alcohol and drugs act in much the same way as caffeine in that they may offer some temporary relief, but they may

cause depression when the effect wears off. They are addictive too, and will further exacerbate any problems that you may have.

- Crying or screaming can often give a release from pent up emotions. In fact, in cases of bereavement crying is an important release, and suppression may lead to the elongation of the mourning process.

Figure 19 is a model that we can use to cope with stress.

We can now go back to the agency and look for signs of stress. Let's look at each character in turn.

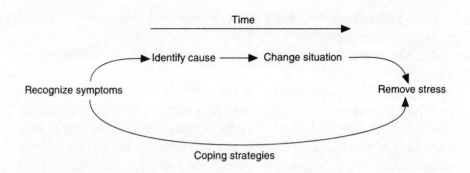

Figure 19 Steps towards eliminating stress

Liz

Liz needs to recognize the symptoms of stress, such as her irritability and rapid mood swings. As a coping strategy she could spend more time with Alan doing the things that they enjoy. Perhaps now that his business is not so busy they could take the opportunity to go on holiday using the cheap flights that Liz is entitled to.

However, none of this will remove the causes of stress, which really come from two areas:

She is working very hard and doing a lot of overtime, partly in order to ensure that she stays on the promotion ladder.

Her next promotion is likely to bring her into even greater conflict with Alan.

The only real way to reduce the stress is to deal with these problems. She and Alan will have to decide where the priorities should lie. Some of the questions they will have to answer are:

Is working long hours the only way to gain promotion?
Could Liz become more effective in her job and therefore reduce the need to work overtime?
How important is promotion to Liz?
How important is Alan's business to Alan (and to Liz)?

Perhaps each of them should carry out personal PEST and SWOT analyses, which we looked at in chapter 2. If each of them has aspirations that are totally incompatible with the other's, then it is perhaps better that they discuss the matter sooner rather than later.

Helen

Helen does not really know where she is going, as we saw in chapter 3 in her conversation with Claire. She has already recognized this and has already taken steps to solve the problem by volunteering to help John.

John

John's stress is being demonstrated by his feelings that everyone must be against him and stems from two areas: his loss of status; lack of confidence in his ability in his new areas of responsibility.

He does not yet seem to have recognized these symptoms. However, he is tackling the latter problem, and if he is successful, this may well raise his own self-esteem and help to alleviate the other problem. John is spending more and more time in his JP duties and this may be one of his ways of coping with stress. On the other hand, these duties may provide him with a good excuse for running away from the place where he feels most stress, and may actually be another symptom of stress.

ACTION PLAN

Now you need to fill in your Action Plan in chapter 10 to help you recognize and deal with stress:

Recognize the symptoms
Make a list of any symptoms of stress that you have.

Devise some ways of coping with stress
List the ways you can reduce your stress levels while you find a solution

Identify the cause of stress
What is the *real* reason for the stress?

Consider options to remove the causes of stress
There may be only one option, but there are likely to be several options which may partially or totally remove the stress. You do need to be careful, however, that your chosen solution does not remove one source of stress and replace it with another. For example, handing your notice in to leave a job that causes you stress may remove that particular cause of stress and replace it with another kind because you can't afford to pay the mortgage now that you are unemployed!

Work towards your preferred option (make the changes)
You may not be able to implement your decision immediately. You may, for example, decide that you need a more challenging job. It is unlikely that you can achieve that immediately. However, once you have decided that is what you want you can start working towards it. You can perhaps learn new skills, or ask to be given tasks that extend your current knowledge and which prepare you for that new job.

ACTION PLAN 12

Now turn to chapter 10 and fill in your stress management action plan.

SUMMARY

In this chapter we have looked at the following issues:

using strategies to avoid conflict
getting to know oneself better
being sensitive to others
being assertive
taking responsibility for your own development
finding the right people to help you
different learning styles
identifying and managing stress

5

How Long will it Take?

'How long will it take?' asked Helen. John had just told her that in addition to a short course on designing questionnaires and interviewing skills, Simon had also arranged that she could go on to the first stage of the company's staff development course. Helen was pleased with the recognition of being offered the course, but apprehensive as to the demands it would make on her leisure time.

'About a year for this part, and then if Head Office agrees you could go on to the next stage, which is an NVQ3 in management.'

'No, what I meant was, how many hours per week will it take me to do the course? I remember that when I was doing my "A" levels I had no time for anything else.'

'Well, Simon said that the course is run on a basis of a workshop every two weeks which takes up an afternoon and an evening. So it is partly in company time, but then there will be an assignment every few weeks plus extra reading and study. On average, he says, it will need about eight hours a week outside work time.'

'I really would like to do it but I don't know how I am going to fit everything in; and I don't want to start it and then have to drop out. I always seem to be short of time as it is.'

'Well, you have been saying that you want to develop a career and this looks like the best option. Whatever course you choose, whether it is in the company or at a college, will require a commitment of time. However, I have got some notes on time management, including an analysis and time planner, in the loft at home, that I could let you have. They were a great help to me when I was trying to juggle my time between managing the three branches, spending time at home with my family, being a JP and still being able to find time to play golf. Eileen and I found that we could cut out lots of things that were wasting our time or were not so important, and rearrange our schedules so that family life didn't suffer.'

As this conversation had taken place in the main office, before the agency opened for the day, it had been overheard by Liz and Sue.

'John, would you mind if I had a look at your notes as well?' asked Liz. 'I am having great difficulty fitting everything in and it is beginning to get me down.'

Before John could think of a good reason why they would not be suitable for Liz, who he did not want to help (see chapter 4), Sue asked if she could also see them as she was about to enrol for the Certificate in Leisure and Tourism course at the local college of further education. She added that as Jason was probably going to take the course too he could also benefit from some guidance on managing time.

'Has anyone had any news on Jason,' asked John, 'I tried to phone his mother last night but there was no answer.'

'I met Paula, his fiancée, this morning on the way to work,' said Sue, 'They think he is alright but are keeping him in for observation. He was banged on the head at football training the night before and they think that it's a bit of concussion.'

'John, if Liz, Helen, Jason and I try to work on our time management problems will you help us?' asked Sue. 'You have already got your time priorities sorted out and I for one will need help if I am to do a full-time job here, manage a home and family and do the course, and would be grateful for the benefit of your experience.'

The others all supported this enthusiastically, and John, who was unaccustomed to being asked by his staff to help in this way, agreed that he would conduct a series of two weekly sessions on the basics of time management. Later, when he was driving home, he realized that whilst it was something he could enter on his next appraisal under the heading of team building, he was actually very pleased to have been asked and felt good about it.

The following week they all gathered in the staff room after the office had closed and Jason had returned from taking mail to the post. Prior to this, John had spent some time going through his notes, as he had not looked at them for several years. He was feeling somewhat apprehensive because he had not done any teaching before, and when he had mentioned this to Eileen, his wife, she had told him that whatever he did he must not appear pompous. He found this to be quite unhelpful and, as she would not elaborate on it, he was left with an uneasy suspicion that perhaps he had been guilty of this in the past, rather like his father used to be.

THINK POINT

Here John has had a part of Johari's Window (see chapter 4) that was previously obscured to him opened up, and it has revealed some baggage that he acquired from his father. What comments have you received recently that might have appeared hurtful at the time but which gave you an insight into how others regard some of your attitudes, actions and habits?

John started off by asking them all to identify the sort of problems that they each had with managing time. No one wanted to be the first to speak up, so John explained that one of his problems, which no doubt they would all agree with, was that however much he tried he always had far too much paper on his desk. This resulted in him spending ages trying to find things, and when he did find whatever he was looking for he would be interrupted and then forget what he had been doing. He added that he used to be like that at home as well, until his wife started to clear his things away so that he could never find them. Sue commented that all husbands must be the same and Liz agreed. John then added that he found that much of his time was taken up with meetings at Head Office which went on and on.

By admitting to his faults John had broken the ice and the others were then prepared to speak up.

Liz was the first, and she commented on the fact that she always wanted to be involved in whatever was going on, and in consequence took far too much upon herself, including things that others were quite capable of doing. She also felt that at home she quickly became bored with mundane jobs like ironing and avoided starting them. When she did get round to them she would suddenly find herself doing something else without consciously deciding to do so. John wrote these onto the flip chart that they used in the office to advertise last-minute reductions in holidays, and asked who was going to be the next. Helen and Sue then started both speaking at the same time and Sue invited Helen to go first.

Helen said she felt that her biggest problem was watching too much television and not getting around to other things unless the impetus came from someone else. Here she contrasted herself with her friend Claire, who was always so full of energy and wanting to do things. She also felt that she became bored very easily when there was time to spare; for example, at lunchtimes on the days when she did not see Claire she usually went back to work early, as she had nothing to do. She also said that she was concerned about the way she started things and then lost interest in them.

Jason commented that it was difficult not to watch television because there was so much good sport on it. He felt that his main trouble at work was in not being able to stop customers 'rabbiting on' while on the telephone and repeating their problems or complaints three times over. The same could be said for customers at the counter who wanted to tell you all about the holidays they have had throughout their lifetimes even when they can see that there is a queue behind them. At home he felt that a large part of his time was taken up with doing jobs around the house that his father 'delegated' to him. (The way he said *delegated* made it sound as though it was one of his father's favourite sayings.) He added that he became irritated with some of the other players in his football team, who claimed that they did not have enough time to attend the training sessions, but they always found enough time to go out socializing.

'Well, I'm last,' said Sue, 'My main problem is that at home I have to be at everyone's beck and call. Because Tony is on shift work he is never available during the week to fetch and take the eldest to cubs or our daughter to her dancing lessons. On Saturday mornings when they want to go over to their friends, who live on a farm, he has to go and get his bait and get his tackle ready for the fishing match on the Sunday when he will be away all day. By the time I have done all of the cooking, washing and clearing up after them all there is no time left for what I want to do. One of the things I like about work is that it gives me a chance to only do three things at once!'

John entered all of these up on the flip chart and pointed out that they would add to the list as they identified more problems.

This is what the sheet looked like:

Name	Problem
John	Disorganized and untidy way of working
	Too many long meetings
Liz	Can't say no to work/needs to feel involved
	Procrastination
	Lack of delegation
Helen	Lack of goals
	Inability to finish things
Jason	Winding up telephone conversations
	Controlling customer interviews
	Father's agenda takes priority
Sue	Can't say no to extra tasks
	Involved in too much for others
	Always puts self last

'It looks to me,' said John, 'as though between us we commit almost every crime in the time management book, and I'm sure we shall find further examples when we analyse how we *actually* spend our time. That's the next step: we think we know how our time is spent but now we need to keep a time diary for two weeks so that we can see where it really does go. For example, I think that too much of my time is taken up in meetings at Head Office, but when I looked in my office diary before we started in here I found that the last one was three weeks ago, whereas I could have sworn that they are at least weekly.'

John then gave them a set of A4 sheets that he had drawn up and photocopied. He explained that they were each to enter all of their activities on the sheets for the next two weeks and that he would do the same. Liz asked whether they were to enter only their leisure activities on the forms; to which John replied that his notes on time management had made it clear that we only have one life and it is impossible to divide it into work and home. He added that a theorist called Likert was quoted as having said that we all have 168 hours per week, but the difference between us is that some people use them more effectively than others. He explained the particular need to ensure that all interruptions, including telephone calls and drop-in visitors, were included.

ACTION PLAN 13

What time management problems do you have? Are they similar to those of our characters or do you have some additional ones? Enter them in your Action Plan in chapter 10.

For the next two weeks keep a time diary in the same way as John, Liz and the others are going to do. Figure 20 is an example of how this should be completed.

Two weeks later when they met after work for their next session there were several glum faces.

'I don't know about the rest of you,' said John, 'but I found it very difficult always to remember to enter my activities on the forms, and when I did forget it was even more difficult to remember everything that had happened during the day.'

There was a general agreement from the others on this; and Sue added that finding time to complete the forms had been a problem in itself.

'My problem,' said Liz, 'was that Alan saw it as more work being done at home and he went mad over it.'

THINK POINT

If Liz had explained to her husband in advance what she was going to do and the possible benefits for home life as well as work, he would probably have been more co-operative and might even have wanted to do something similar. What similar situations occur in your life where discussing things openly could lead to a more positive response?

```
┌─────────────────────────────────────────────────────────────┐
│                                                               │
│   Time Diary                                                  │
│                                                               │
│                                                               │
│   Day ..................................   Date ........................................   Page no .............   │
│                                                               │
│                                                               │
│   Activity                       Start    End    Duration    Comments   │
│                                                               │
│                                                               │
│                                                               │
│                                                               │
│                                                               │
│                                                               │
│                                                               │
│                                                               │
│                                                               │
│                                                               │
│                                                               │
│                                                               │
│                                                               │
│                                                               │
│                                                               │
│                                                               │
│                                                               │
│                                                               │
│                                                               │
│                                                               │
│                                                               │
│                                                               │
│                                                               │
│                                                               │
│                                                               │
└─────────────────────────────────────────────────────────────┘
```

Figure 20 Sample time diary page

John then explained that the next step was to analyse the data they had created so that they could see how much time they were spending on the different activities.

'There are obviously any number of different categories you can use and they will vary from person to person. For example, I shall have a total for all of the activities relating to being a JP – such as getting ready, travelling to and from the court, actually hearing the cases, telephone calls and administration, discussions with colleagues, reading and any training sessions. It is far more than just the few hours a fortnight that I spend actually hearing cases. However, we all have some categories in common, and if we do those first we can discuss them as we go.'

John then listed on the flip chart the heading *sleep*.

'I think we need to make this include the period from getting ready for bed until we are up and dressed the next morning, rather than just the time we are asleep.'

'How do we count the time if we always read in bed?' asked Helen.

'Well, it depends on whether you read for a long time or not. If it's less than half an hour you can leave it as part of sleep; but if it's more, then that time needs to be counted as a different activity. If you are reading a novel or something for recreational purposes then count it under that category when we come to it, but if it's something to do with your course then count it under that instead.'

The next heading John wrote up was *work at home*.

'By this I don't mean the office work that I sometimes do at home, as I call that "work work",' said John. 'What I mean is all the other jobs, like housework, cutting the grass, cleaning the car, preparing meals, paying bills, decorating, gardening, etc. If you do any other sort of "work" at home, like Sue's committee work for the PTA or organizing a football team like Jason does, it would be as well to have a separate category for that. And if things like gardening, sewing and carpentry are hobbies then leave them out of the figures for this heading, as they are things that you want to do rather than have to do. Where they are jobs that are more or less the same amount of time each week we can use the figures from your diary analysis, but things like gardening are seasonal.

For most people, there's not much to do after clearing up the leaves in October/November until tidying up and starting grass cutting in March/April – apart from a bit of pruning, that is. Decorating is even more of a problem, as it may only be one or two weekends a year. There is no guidance in the notes how to account for these, so what I suggest is that we treat these in a different way. If we identify each of the activities that are seasonal or have an irregular time commitment, and the weeks in the year when they will probably take place, we can then estimate what the commitment will be for those weeks, and we will know that we have to budget for that many extra hours for those weeks only. This may mean that we have to decide well in advance when we are going to do the decorating, but at least if we have put it in our diaries we can make sure that we have prepared for it by, say, choosing and ordering the paper sufficiently in advance so that we are not held up when we are ready to do it. It's actually a lot like spending money. You have a lot more expenditure for summer holidays and Christmas and you have to budget for it.

Those of us with gardens will have to allow a number of hours per week from the middle of March to the middle of November with extra in April to June.'

John then looked at the clock and suggested that as the time was nearing 6 p.m. and the calculations for that part were all on an individual basis, they should do them at home and bring them to the next session. This they agreed to do.

At their next session they used the first part of the time in discussing the number of hours each of them spent under the first two headings of *sleep* and *work at home*.

'We had better have *committee work* as the next heading so that we don't forget it,' said John, as he added it to the list on the flip chart.

'This one is more difficult,' said Sue. 'Over the two weeks of my diary analysis there wasn't any PTA work, whereas some weeks when we have a fund-raising event it can take up to two or three evenings and all of the Saturday plus the clearing up on a Sunday morning.'

'I have the same problem with my football, as it only runs from the beginning of September through to the middle of May,' Jason added before John could reply.

'Yes, we are all faced with that sort of problem, as there is not such a thing as a typical week,' replied John. 'Some things like my magistrate work are quite regular and so are easy to put down.

But if Sue deals with her PTA work in the same way as we did for decorating, and you deal with your football in the same way as we discussed for gardening, then that should cover it. Oh, and Jason do be sure that you only put down the organizing or admin part of your football and not the training or playing, as they come somewhere else. We all need to be careful, though, that we put down all of the things we get involved with over the year. I found that I had forgotten some because they only happen at certain times of the year, such as the Christmas carol concert and the Travel Agents Association golf day, both of which I help to arrange.'

Liz, Sue and Jason all had calculations to do under this heading, and John had already done his, but Helen felt left out and was a bit ashamed to admit that she did not do anything. She mentioned this to the others, but they pointed out that they had all taken on these commitments because they wanted to, for whatever reasons, and that it was up to her how she chose to spend her time. She still felt that she would like to be involved in something and decided that she would discuss it with Claire when they met later that evening.

'The next section is what I call *"work work"*,' said John, as he wrote it on the flip chart. 'It's the time taken for our jobs here, and needs to include getting ready to come, the travel time, the time here and getting changed when we get home, plus any extra work that we do in our time for the company.'

'You mean like writing that blasted report for Simon and my course,' asked Liz.

'The report, yes, but your course no,' said John. 'Your course is something you want to do as part of your personal development, and we shall have a separate heading for that later on.'

'What do we do about lunch hours?' asked Helen.

'Treat them in a similar way to what we have just done over reading in bed, depending on how you use them. Do remember, though, that lunch hours can be good times for doing the small jobs that take a long time if you have to come into town specially for them, such as some items of shopping or visiting the library. They can also be a good time for studying.'

The total for this heading was an easier one to calculate and they were soon ready to move on. However, John reminded them that like *work at home* the data would need more analysis later on so that they could see how much time their various duties took up.

The next heading John wrote up was *personal development*.

'This includes far more than any study or courses that you are doing. It can include things like keep-fit, football training, golf coaching, reading or Sue's work on the PTA. It depends why you are doing it, and only you can answer that. In my case I have set myself the goal of getting my golf handicap down to 12 by the end of next summer, and I am having coaching from the club professional. Also, I have realized that I was put off from Shakespeare and the classics at school, so I have now set myself the task of catching up after all these years. Whilst I am enjoying it, I still see it as personal development because it results from a personal development goal I set myself. In the same way if Sue's involvement in the PTA or Jason's football training result from wanting to improve or develop in some way, then that time would come under this heading. If Jason attends football training just because he likes it, then it would come under *leisure*. Whilst it doesn't apply to anyone here, if someone was attending one of these slimming clubs that time would be also be personal development.

Well, having already mentioned it several times, our next and possibly last heading is *leisure*. However, I think it would be a good idea if we have separate totals for things we do a lot (like me with my golf), and also a separate total for watching TV and listening to music.'

After they had completed the figures for this section John then asked them whether they had any items left that required an additional category.

Helen pointed out that she had not put the time taken for meals into any category, and Sue asked where she should put going to church.

'Let's take Helen's point first,' said John. 'It's another of those "depends" ones. If you're having a social meal with family or friends then I think it should come under *leisure*. However if it is a quick meal because of the need to eat, then I suggest we put it under *work at home*. What do you think?'

They all agreed to this, although Liz said that she would have difficulty going back over her time diary to work out which category it came under, as she had not thought to make notes of whether Alan was there or not.

THINK POINT

This is the first time during these sessions that John has asked them what they think. It's a pity that he has not done it more, as it can help to retain people's interest and gain their commitment. Unfortunately in this case he has told them what he thinks first, which could well influence their response. How often do you ask your team for their views, and do you let them know what you think before or afterwards?

John then turned to Sue's query. 'This is up to you. You can either include it in *leisure* as that should include all of the things that you do because you want to for your own sake; or you can show it under a separate heading.'

'I think that I would rather it was a separate heading, as it seems wrong to mix it in with leisure activities.'

'Right, we will do that. The totals should add up to 336 hours, as we looked at two weeks, so if we divide each total by two we can see what our weekly figures look like. What surprises can anyone see in their figures?'

There was quiet for several minutes as though no one wanted to be the first to speak. Then Liz, who had been very careful to keep quiet during these sessions so that the others felt more able to speak, decided that it was necessary to help John out by volunteering her thoughts.

THINK POINT

It would be very easy for a confident person like Liz who is senior to the others to feel that she has to speak most of the time to show that she knows what it is all about. What Liz has done by being quiet and unobtrusive up until now shows far more maturity and thought for others. She is also quite right to help out now when the others are feeling shy about talking about their results. What would you have done in this situation?

'What surprises me about my results is that they show that I have 19 hours of leisure time per week. Before we did this exercise I would have guessed that I only had about an hour per day, and that is when I am so tired that I don't feel like doing anything with it. One thing that I am sure of is that as soon as we can afford it I am going to employ someone to do the cleaning one morning a week, as I hate cleaning and it puts me in a thoroughly bad mood – as Alan knows to his cost.'

This admission by Liz prompted several of the others to start talking at the same time and John had to ask them to speak one at a time. After a pause Jason was the first to speak.

'My results show that I don't spend much time at home and my dad demands a lot of that.'

'How many hours a week does your father take up for jobs at home?' asked Sue.

'Well, about eight hours a week.'

'Do you have to pay full rent at home or do you think that your father sees those eight hours as a part of your contribution to family life?'

'I pay quite a lot, but not as much as Helen pays in rent.'

'I don't only have to pay for the rent of my flat, I have to find the money for all the bills and food on top of that,' exclaimed Helen. 'You don't know when you are well off!'

'Now, now,' said Sue. 'He very soon will, now that he is engaged to be married. The big question is, Jason, can you see where the time will come from to do your course?'

'I suppose that if I don't see Paula the evening I go to college and I miss some TV I should be able to fit it in.'

'You're lucky; according to my calculations, I only have two or three hours a week to myself, so I can't see how I am going to get to college for an evening let alone do any homework,' said Sue, looking quite despondent. 'I thought that by just working harder I would be able to create more time for my course, but this has shown me that I am already over-committed.'

The others started to commiserate with Sue, but John interrupted them. 'Hang on a minute, all I asked was what surprises can you see in your totals of how you use your time. It's too soon to start making assumptions as to whether you can do a course or whatever else you might want to do. Remember each of us already uses up our full quota of 168 hours per week, even if it is only for unimportant things. Whatever extra we choose to do has got to be in place of something we already do. Like Jason not seeing Paula for one evening and watching less TV.'

'But I don't have things like that to give up. I have to look after the home and family, and do the cooking and cleaning and gardening.'

Again John had to interrupt Sue who was getting quite heated as she was now certain that she would be unable to take her course in leisure and tourism. John realized that he needed to get them back to methodically working through their analyses, but he first had to find an answer to satisfy Sue for the time being.

'Look what we put on the flip chart for you, Sue, when we listed our time management problems.

Sue   Can't say no to extra tasks
                Involved in too much for others
                Always puts self last

Those problems are linked to the work that you have at home, and to a certain extent here also, as we all get you to do things for us. We will look at those and at all of the problems we put on the flip chart next time, after we have completed our analysis. Okay?

Right, does everyone have a total for the next two weeks of about 336 hours? Yes? Well now let's move on to the next step. We need to carry out a further analysis of some of the categories, and as you are all concerned about finding time outside work hours for college courses and study, I suggest that we look at all of them apart from "*work work*". We need to break the totals down still further so that you can see how many hours per week is taken up by Sue in ferrying her kids to and from their clubs, etc., and how long Liz takes in preparing meals or doing the housework. It's only when we have a more detailed breakdown that we can help one another to find shortcuts and alternatives. I suggest that as it has gone six o'clock you break the figures down as far as you can before we meet in two weeks' time. Now, on a totally different subject, would you all like to join me for a drink over at the Falcon?'

Apart from staff meetings it was unusual for all of John's staff to be together, as most of the time they were serving the customers. John took the opportunity created by their time management session to suggest that they go out on a social basis, even if it was only for a quick drink before going home. Actually this was something that he had not previously done apart from at Christmas, and it was a comment after the previous session from his wife Eileen that prompted him to do so now.

THINK POINT

One of the reasons why people enjoy or dislike working somewhere is based on how they get on with their colleagues and the social atmosphere that exists there. The occasional get-together where everyone is on equal terms can be a very important aid to team building. How often do you and your team get together socially, and when was the last time?

SUMMARY

This chapter is the first of two that look at how we use our time.

We have seen how a series of team-building meetings happened partly by chance and partly on the initiative of a member of staff who felt able to ask her manager for help. This serves to remind us that managers do not have a monopoly on good ideas. But staff need to feel confident that they will be listened to before they will speak out.

They have spent some time in identifying time management problems, which they are proposing to deal with later, when the diary analyses are complete.

The diary analyses have given each of them an opportunity to look at how they spend their 168 hours per week, and the evidence of the analysis has caused them some surprises.

The way in which we spend our time tends to vary as time goes on, and it is useful to carry out a diary analysis exercise once a year. A good way of remembering to do this is to use the same period each year, such as the fortnight after your birthday.

It is not necessary to analyse your time in exactly the same way as our characters. You may require more or less detail in yours, but do try to be consistent in your approach.

In your analysis try not to forget those items in your life that are seasonal but take up a lot of time.

We have seen how Sue leaped to the conclusion that she would be unable to take her course through lack of time, without considering whether it was more important than some of her present use of her time.

Finally, we have seen how John, prompted by his wife, has suggested that they finish on a social note.

6
Finding the Time

When they met at their next session two weeks later John asked them if they would mind entering their totals against the categories he had written up on the flip chart.

'Please don't feel that you have to if you don't want to; but I think it will help all of us if we can see how differently we use our time.'

No one appeared to be at all concerned about showing their totals to the others, and they all entered them on the chart. This is what it looked like:

	Sleep	Work at home	Committee	Personal development	'Work work'	Leisure	Spiritual
John	56	18	6	12	49	Golf 12 TV 8 Other 6	–
Liz	52½	28	3	12	55	TV 7 Other 12	–
Sue	59½	48	6 (average)	–	48	TV 2½	4
Helen	66	16	–	–	45	TV 22 Other 18	–
Jason	49	13	8	12	45	F'bll 10 TV 15 Other 16	–

'Let's just look at the main differences in the figures. I know that at our second meeting we discussed the first two categories, but it will probably help if we go over the differences there again.

Under the heading of *sleep*, I said that I get up early on Sundays to play golf so that I am back home by 12.30 p.m. Liz said that she goes to bed late most nights but sleeps in on Sundays. Sue told us that her figures for sleep are influenced by the fact that she is so tired after working for so many hours each day that she goes to bed early. Helen mentioned that she likes to sleep in on a Sunday morning and often goes to bed early during the week to save on heating in her flat. She also said that she takes a long time over her hair and make-up in the morning. Jason felt that his figures for sleep were very low because he goes to bed very late and never stays in bed late on Sundays because of football. Actually, Jason, if you look at your figures, bearing in mind that they include getting dressed and undressed and washing, etc., you don't appear to get enough sleep.'

'I find that if I go to bed earlier,' said Jason, 'I just lay there for hours wide awake; but if I go to bed late I fall asleep straight away.'

'Well, you never look tired and washed out as I would be if I had so little sleep,' said Helen.

'The second category, as I recall, we only mentioned briefly at our second session as we said we would come back to it when we had carried out a more detailed analysis – which we have now done. Obviously there are wide differences between our figures, and it will probably help if we have a separate chart showing the breakdown so that we can discuss them. I shall only have space for six headings but we can break our figures down further within those.'

	Housework Shopping Laundry	Cooking Washing up Eating	WORK AT HOME Repairs Sewing	Gardening Car cleaning	Paperwork (bills etc.)	DIY Decorating
John	1 Shpg	3 Ckg 2 WU 6 Eating	½	4 Grdng ½ Car	1	–

'The figure I have put in for eating is only part of the time taken over meals each week, as I have included breakfasts during the week as a part of going to work, so it is under *work work*, and more relaxed family meals are under *leisure*,' John explained.

'What's the three hours for cooking and two hours for washing up, John?' asked Sue.

'Well, I buy the food and cook the dinner on Saturdays, which I enjoy doing, and we have an arrangement whereby it's my job to do the pots and load and unload the dishwasher. Anyway, let's get the rest of the figures entered first and then discuss them.'

They all entered their figures under those that John had already put up for himself.

	Housework Shopping Laundry	Cooking Washing up Eating	WORK AT HOME Repairs Sewing	Gardening Car cleaning	Paperwork (bills etc.)	DIY Decorating
John	1 Shpg	3 Ckg 2 WU 6 Eating	½	4 Grdng ½ Car	1	–
Liz	3 Hsewk 3 Shpg 3 Ldry	10 Ckg 4 WU 4 Eating	–	–	1	–
Sue	5 Hsewk 7 Shpg 6 Ldry 5 Ferrying and waiting for kids.	12 Ckg 5 WU 2 Eating	3	1½ Grdng	½	1 (average)
Helen	2 Hsewk 2 Shpg 2 Ldry	4 Ckg 1½ WU 4½ Eating	–	–	–	–
Jason	–	5 Eating	1	4 Grdng 1 Car	–	2

'Let's start at the top and work our way through,' said John.

'Why is there nothing against decorating or DIY on yours, John? I can remember you coming in laden with wallpaper and paints on several occasions,' asked Liz.

'I'm sorry,' said John. 'I should have mentioned earlier that the figure I have put down for gardening is for what I do during the gardening season, not an average throughout the year. I did it this way because it is at the same time of the year that I play the most golf. When I don't have to do the garden it gives me the time to do the decorating and repairs, so I have not put anything against them. When I can't play golf it gives me more time for reading and other leisure things.'

'Oh, well, I need to alter mine in the same way,' said Sue. 'That way I should have two and a half hours a week for gardening and nothing for decorating. What about you, Jason, is yours the same?'

'No, mine is alright. Because of the greenhouse and the conservatory I have gardening to do throughout the year. The only difference is that the figures are round the other way in winter – two hours gardening and four hours decorating and DIY.'

John realized that the session was in danger of being taken up with trivia relating to small differences in the ways that they had used the categories, whereas it was each individual's use of their time that was important.

'I think we shall take up too much time if we look at each figure for all five of us. Let's concentrate on those areas where there are possible savings to be made and the problems we listed during our first session. For example, I recognize that I have got to be much more organized and tidy in the way I work, and I am going to set myself a goal based on that. I shall put review dates in my diary to check progress, and now that we have discussed it I shall also be conscious that you will all be watching the state of my desk to see whether I slip back again.

Liz, you mentioned the other week that you wanted a cleaner as soon as you could afford one, but the figures don't show many hours of work to make one worthwhile, do they?'

'No, I have been looking at that and I think that the things you hate doing the most always seem to take so much longer. Instead I am going to invest in a dishwasher. Some of the time that I have put down under cooking is actually spent in washing up the things I have used in preparing the meals. I have also decided that when I can I am going to buy a small television so that I can watch TV and do the ironing at the same time. Between them they should give me another five hours a week.'

'That's fine, but what about the items we put down on the first chart, the problem areas?'

'Well, we have not got onto the 'work work' category yet, which is where most of the problems are; and the 'procrastination' one is mostly about doing the ironing and the housework. The ironing I have already mentioned, and the housework does not take as long as I thought it does.'

'I don't mind the housework,' said Sue. 'I borrow my son's walkman and listen to the radio whilst I'm doing mine.'

'This is getting expensive. I now need a walkman as well as a dishwasher and portable television. But joking apart it's a good idea.'

'Are there any jobs that you insist on doing that your husband might want to share in?' asked John, 'like the budgets and bills?'

'I doubt it, as he would like me to do far more of his company's bookkeeping and he has no love of paperwork. I do see what you mean though. The fact that I like to be involved in everything at work suggests that I may be the same at home. I shall have to give it some thought, and I may even ask Alan what he thinks.'

'Right, Sue is next. What ideas have you had, Sue, since you saw the breakdown of your figures?'

'I just don't know where to begin. All I can see is that for me to do a course at all, then sacrifices would have to be made by Tony and the kids, and I can't see that happening.'

'Okay, well let's all see what we can suggest to help you. We will have a brain-storming for the remainder of this session to come up with as many ideas as possible for you, and then you can think about them before our next session and tell us what you have decided.'

Sue rather dubiously agreed to this, and found herself being swept along by the others in a light-hearted brain-storming session which lasted about ten minutes. The ideas varied from resigning from the PTA to persuading Tony to find a job that did not involve shift work. Sue collected up the sheets on which these suggestions had been listed and promised that she would find the time to study them before the next session.

The following week when they gathered in the staff room for their next session a very much more cheerful Sue reported that she and her husband Tony had spent time together going through the suggestions. They had agreed to implement some straight away and others as soon as practicable. She had been very surprised to find that Tony could quite easily find time on Saturdays to take the children to their friends' and collect them later on. He had also suggested that when he was on the early shift he could take and collect their son from cubs. They had been out that week and bought a dishwasher and it was now the children's job to load and unload it. Also they had decided that after three years on the PTA committee it was time that someone else took a turn, so Sue would be resigning at the annual general meeting next month. They calculated that these changes could average about twelve hours per week; but six hours of this related to the PTA, which was not every week. They had therefore decided that when Sue's mother retired in two months' time they would pay her to come round to their house, on Wednesday afternoons, and do the laundry for them. She would then be there with the children whilst Sue went to College. Sue's mother was very happy with the proposal because it gave her some extra income as well as a chance to have her grandchildren to herself.

This would relieve Sue of most of the six hours per week that she spent on washing and ironing at present.

'You don't think your mother would like to take on mine as well?' asked Liz.

'No, I don't, you will have to find someone else. But you do only take up three hours per week for washing and ironing. Oh! I forgot: we are also going to try to do a big shop, as a family, once a month for the non-perishables. That will save me some time each week, as I can buy the perishable stuff during my lunch hours. We reckon that most weeks will have a saving of two hours, but with no saving the week we do the big shop. But as the whole family will be doing it, there will be no increase in my time.'

'Right,' said John, 'that looks very satisfactory, Sue, and goes to show what is possible when you take a good look at the figures and the alternatives.'

THINK POINT

John is, of course, right in what he has just said, but just as important in Sue's success in finding economies in her time usage has been the support given by her husband, children and her mother, and the ideas of the other members of her work team. As you will recall, we discussed the need to identify who can help us with our goals, and this is a good time to have another look at what you recorded in your action plan for this.

'Now we need to look at Helen's figures to see what help she needs.'

'Well I don't think that I need any help, as the diary analysis makes it quite clear that I have plenty of time for anything that I really want to do. I feel so guilty that it was me complaining about being short of time that started these sessions off, when I'm the one with the most time available. It has made it even clearer to me that I need to set some goals in my life. I seem to be frittering it away at present.'

'Hang on,' said John, 'there is no law that says you have got to be working or doing something "constructive" for the whole time, and we have all benefited from these sessions, so we ought to be thanking you. Also, we all need relaxation and unwinding periods, and different people use them in different ways.'

'Well, I know that I have the time to do my course, and I am looking to get on the committee of the ski club so that I can become more involved. Which could, of course, be good for business.'

'That's great if it is what *you* want to do and it is important to you, but it must be your agenda and not because other people want you to do it. After all, it's your life. It does, however, bring me to a key concept in time management – that of importance versus urgency. As we have already found, we only have 168 hours per week and we need to use them as effectively as possible. That means prioritizing those things that are the most important because that's where our main results and satisfaction come from. Other jobs may be urgent but not at all important, so we need to do them first but not take very long over them. That way we can leave more time for the important things – important to us that is. We can even give all of the jobs that we need to do ratings on a scale of 1 to 10 for their importance and for their urgency, and decide in what order to do them and how long to allow. One way of doing this is to plot them on a chart like this.' John then drew the figure on the flip chart (figure 21).

'Jason, that leaves you; and you have already said that you can fit in your course if you watch less television and don't see Paula on college nights. But what other changes, if any, do you want to make in your use of time?'

'Well, for a start I can now see that I do 8 hours per week doing the jobs my dad wants me to do, and that's not much seeing how little I pay to live at home. I have also realized that I am using 30 hours per week on football between the committee work, training and actually playing, and that has got to be too much. Paula and I looked at my figures and agreed that it would be unfair for me to carry on at that level after we are married. In fact it is unfair now, as I give more time to football than I do to her, and she has admitted that she feels a bit resentful at times. I just seem to have taken on more and more of the work as no one else would do it. What we have decided is that next season I am only prepared to do one or two of the jobs out of captain, secretary/treasurer and fixtures secretary that I do now. The 12 hours I spend on training and keeping fit I am going to alter so that I go to football training once a week from September to May, and Paula and I go the fitness centre once a week together.'

'That sounds fine, Jason. It looks as though we have all given some serious thought to the *work at home* section, but we will need to talk about it again in, say, a month's time, to see if it is all working out as we have planned. I think we can leave you all to look at any other adjustments you need to make.

We can now concentrate on the time we spend here at work, or the *work work* section of our time analyses, as that was the other area where we said that we would need to break the figures down more thoroughly. This will be more difficult, because Liz and I have different duties from the rest of you. However, we can start off with breaking the figures down into a few general categories that are common to us all.

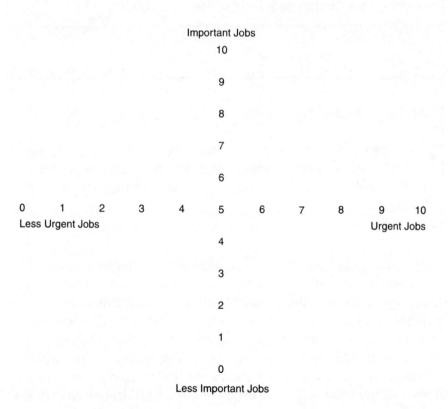

Figure 21 Urgency chart

THINK POINT

Here once again we can see the advantages of bringing things out into the open and discussing them with those who are affected by our actions and decisions. Jason has found out how Paula feels about the amount of time his football takes up and they have identified a satisfactory solution. This would certainly have been a potential source of aggravation after they were married. We can see evidence in this chapter of how John and his wife Eileen, Sue and her husband Tony, and Jason and his fiancée Paula have discussed their use of time and have arrived at amicable alternatives. This is not the case with Liz and her husband Alan, who have not yet discussed and reached agreement over Liz's career needs – an omission which in many cases would jeopardize the relationship.

ACTION PLAN 14

Are there any aspects of your life that might cause resentment to your partner, and are they aware of your aspirations? If so, add them to your action plan in chapter 10 now.

'We mentioned when we were working out the total hours that we spend at work that we would include the time we take to get ready for work and the travelling time to and from work, so we will use that as the first subheading. Next, we all spend time doing work for customers and we can divide that into bookings, queries and telephone calls. The customer bookings and queries headings are for the ones where the customer is here in the office. If we use the total length of time we are with the customer it will include any telephone calls that we make during that interview. The other heading for telephone calls is for incoming and outgoing calls, and can cover all of the remaining telephone calls, including the queries received by telephone. For the remaining headings we all have to do some form of administration, such as finishing the paperwork after the customer has gone and sending out the final invoices, confirmations, tickets, etc.; so we will make that as heading. Those of us on the counter have tea and coffee breaks, so that can be another one. Any duties that do not fit into the categories we have listed so far can be lumped under "Other Duties' for the time being.

If we all spend a few minutes analysing our data under those headings we can see how they compare.'

When they were all ready John entered the results on the flip chart.

	Getting ready & travel	Customer bookings	Customer queries	Telephone calls	Admin	Breaks	Others duties	Total
John	7	10	8	7	10	–	7	49
Liz	8	10	8	6	10	–	13	55
Sue	10½	18	4	2	4	2½	7	48
Helen	10	18	6	2½	4	2½	2	45
Jason	10	14	6	3	5	2½	4	45

'If we deduct the first column from the last one we can see how many hours we spend actually working. The fact that Liz and I have more than the rest of you is quite reasonable. I did not realize, though, Liz, that you did so many more than I do.'

'That's a result of the work that I take home to do,' said Liz. 'I find it easier to do the monthly figures and reports at home where there are no interruptions.'

'That's alright on odd occasions,'said John, 'but you should not make a habit of it. We will come to that when we look at our individual problems. The other figure that stands out from the hours at work is that Sue is doing extra time when we know that she can least spare it.'

'Well, I am still trying to get the hang of the new computerized airline booking system,' said Sue, 'and the paperwork from the holiday bookings always takes me longer than it does Helen and Jason.'

'I will give you some training on any areas of the computer bookings you are not sure about,' said Liz; 'but really your only problem with the holiday bookings is that you don't trust yourself enough: there is nothing wrong with your work when you have completed it, and yet you still check it several times more.'

'Hopefully we have just found you another two and a half hours a week,' said John.

'We shall need to carry out more analysis of the time we spend on the different sorts of customer bookings, queries and telephone calls. And we need to know on average how long it takes each of us to carry out the different sorts of transactions. I know that each case is different and depends on the customer and the length of time it takes to get through on the telephone to tour operators, etc., but that is why I am suggesting that we look at average times. Rather than doing that as a part of these meetings I think it will be better if I see each of you individually, during office time, to go through your figures with you.

What I would like to do now is to look at the time management problems that we each identified in our first session. Many of them related to problems at work, and we can not only learn from another's mistakes but we can also give support to each other when we are trying to change any bad habits, and so forth. I don't think it should take long, as we have already covered a number of them.

If we work our way through the list we made on the flip chart, mine came first, and we can see that I identified two main problems [back near the beginning of chapter 5] – a disorganized and untidy way of working, and too many long meetings. The first of these I have been trying to do something about, and several of you have helped me with your reminders when I have forgotten; and the second one is actually nowhere near as bad as it seemed to be before I did my diary analysis.'

'Your desk is certainly much clearer, John,' said Sue; 'and what's more you can use your wardrobe for its proper purpose now that you have got rid of all of the paper from it.'

'That's right, some of that paper went back five years. Liz, you are next. What are we going to do about your problems?'

'Well, mine were, "can't say no to work/needs to feel involved", "procrastination" and "lack of delegation". I think there is a link between the first one and the third one, and now that I am conscious of them I am trying to pass more on to train the others. I used to have the idea that it is always quicker to do things yourself, and it can be if it is just a one off; but training others to do things is an investment, and I know that that is what

I should be doing. Saying no to work is proving more difficult, as I suppose that I have always been like that, and it will take a lot more time and effort to change me. The procrastination one was over the mundane jobs at home and I am dealing with those. I don't think that I put off doing things here, do I?'

As there was an embarrassed silence at this point, Liz blushed and then laughed. 'Okay, so which jobs do I put off here?'

'Well, recently there was that report for the Area Manager, and you always put off phoning Head Office for as long as possible,' said Sue.

'Oh, that report needed a clear run at it without any interruptions, but I agree about the phone calls.'

'We were very quiet on the Thursday afternoon as usual, and John was out, so I suggested to you that you used his office to work on the report, but you came and talked to us on the counter instead.'

'Okay, you win, it's another development need I have and one you can all help me with.'

THINK POINT

If we go back to Liz's inability to say no to work, and her need to feel involved, this is a very common situation. Usually it relates to our formative years when we wanted to please parents and other adults including, our first teachers. As a result it becomes habitual. It therefore forms part of the baggage that Liz is carrying, and is a part of her behaviour that needs modifying so that she does not become over-committed. Try to view your own behaviour as though you were seeing yourself on video – do you go over the top in trying to please partners, parents, line-managers, etc.; and do you feel guilty when you are unable to help them?

'Can we just focus on that report for a moment Liz?' said John. 'It is an example of a useful point in time management. You said that you needed a clear run at it. Clearing a big piece of time is never easy in our type of work, and I have found that if you are not careful those sort of jobs finish up by being done by staying late after work, or are taken home, as you have already mentioned that you do. My time management notes suggest that a big job like a report can be broken down into a series of small jobs. It's called "chunking". When you get a job like that report to do you need to start by making out a file with a sheet of paper attached to the front of it. On the sheet of paper you break down all of the steps that need to be taken and then set deadlines for each of them. That way you can do some of the shorter ones in between your own jobs. For example, if your report was on, say, how package holiday sales to Spain this summer compared in numbers and income per resort with last year: you would need to break the job down into, say, getting out last year's file, finding the figures you needed there, summarizing this year's figures, comparing the two sets of figures, calculating the percentage differences, finding out the reasons for any major changes, drafting your report, checking your report and sending it. Some of the jobs you could get others to do for you. Whilst writing the report sounds the biggest job, actually it's getting all of the information together and in the right order that takes the most time. However, you do have to make a vow that you will cross one of the jobs off every time you pick the file up. That way you overcome any tendency to procrastinate by picking it up and putting it down because you would rather do something else.

Actually, "chunking" works for jobs at home as well, such as completing your income tax return or decorating a room or painting the outside of the house. Those of you who are doing courses may find it useful when you have assignments to write.'

'Alright, I'll try that in future, and perhaps it will improve the climate at home. Alan hates to see me doing office work, unless it's his,' said Liz.

'Before we leave your time management problems I think it would be a good idea if we spent a few minutes talking about delegation. Liz had identified that she has a problem in being able to make herself delegate, and Jason and Sue have both identified similar problems out of work. Jason's is with his football club responsibilities, and Sue up until now has kept all of the jobs at home to herself and is surprised to learn that her husband and her children are quite ready to take some of them off her. I am also prepared to bet that it is the same in her work with the Parent Teachers Association.'

Sue nodded her agreement to this.

'If we look at delegation purely in a work context for the moment, you can then apply the same principles to your other activities. Liz said a few minutes ago that she realized that she used to have the idea that it is always quicker to do things yourself, but she can now see that this is wrong. That is one of the commonest reasons for people not delegating. Another is that they feel that they are too busy to explain it to someone else. Sometimes people keep jobs to themselves because they like doing them, or they have a fear of losing control, or they are afraid that they will appear less important or less busy. Often it is because they see their subordinates as already having a full work-load and do not want to add to it.

THINK POINT

As a result of the sessions and the fact that Liz has maintained a similar profile to the others, John appears to be less antagonistic towards her and is treating her the same way as his other staff. This is because she is willing to learn from him and is doing it jointly with the others and not in a 'pushy way', so he does not feel threatened by her. How comfortable is your line manager with you? Do you think that he or she feels threatened at times by your reactions to situations?

'It is necessary to ask yourself five questions:

What should I delegate?
To whom should I delegate it?
Are they capable of learning to do it?
How much training will they need?
What would the benefits be?

You need to remember that although you are delegating the authority and responsibility for doing the task, you are still accountable for it, as it is a part of your job that is being delegated. So you need to monitor that it is being done correctly and that any deadlines are being met. In Jason's case it looks as though he has taken on a number of different roles and has amalgamated them. So in his case if someone else is appointed by the club to take on the role of, say, secretary/treasurer, then he would not still be accountable for it – they would become accountable to the committee in his place. Whereas if someone simply gave him a hand with that aspect of his responsibilities he would retain his accountability to the committee for the work being done.

When a task is delegated the person who takes it on very often gets upset if their manager – or whoever gave them the task – checks up to see how it is going. They complain that if the person does not trust them to do it they should not have given it to them in the first place. This simply shows that it was not delegated properly. The person who is delegating it should make it clear from the outset how much training will be given, when they will be expected to do the work without supervision, and the level of monitoring that will take place and why. They may also set some goals with clearly defined levels of performance so that they can both see how it is progressing. That way there are no surprises when monitoring takes place, and it can be discussed quite openly.

The benefits of delegating are that the work that is done by the more senior members of staff is usually more important in terms of the business. So by doing more of the important things it helps to grow the business. Obviously anything that Liz and I delegate cannot be more important than serving the customers, but it could be more important than some of the things you have listed under extra duties. Also, the work that is delegated to us, including the work that Simon delegates to Liz and me, can help us to develop new skills and experience and make the job more interesting. An example of this is where Simon wants me to organize a campaign to gain a major share of the business travel from the firms who are moving into the area. Helen has kindly offered to help me, so I shall be delegating part of the work to her; but Simon will still be holding me accountable for it. As he has delegated it to me he will be checking to see how it is progressing, and I shall be discussing progress on a regular basis with Helen so that we both know how the other is getting on. I will be able to get help from Simon, who has done this sort of thing before, and both Helen and I will benefit from the new experience of running this sort of campaign. I hope that there will be times when the rest of you will be able to help us.'

ACTION PLAN 15

What jobs do you need to delegate? Make a list of them in your action plan in chapter 10 and the name or names of the person or people to whom you can delegate them. Next make a note of any training that they will require and the likely time-scales. Finally, identify what the benefits would be.

'Are there any questions on delegations before we move on?

No? Well if you think of any we can always discuss them at our next staff meeting. Helen, you were next on our chart of time management crimes; what have you to say for yourself?'

'Well, I think that I have already covered my admitted failings,' replied Helen. 'I have now started to set some goals in areas that really interest me, so I think that I shall see them through. But I know that I will need someone to keep an eye on me just as my Mum used to do, so that I don't slip back.'

'I think we will all need to help one another for some time to come,' said John. 'What I propose is that we spend ten minutes reporting on our progress at our monthly staff meeting, but that we mention anything that we see where one of us is going wrong whenever it happens.'

THINK POINT

It is very difficult to change long-established habits, particularly if they are part of the baggage we have picked up in childhood. We therefore need help and feedback from someone we can trust, and this is a good time for you to identify the person or people who can do this for you (and enter it in your action plan in chapter 10).

'Jason, you were next. You had three problems, the first two of which related to work.'

'Yes, the first two were about not being able to keep customer telephone calls short, and customers on the counter going on and on. The third one was about the work my Dad wants me to do, and we have covered that.'

'Right, the first two are really down to experience. Obviously we want all of our customers to feel that they are the most important, and one of the things with the telephone is for them to feel that the sooner they hang up the sooner you can do what they want, whether it is making a booking or obtaining information, and so on. What I suggest is that you listen in to suitable calls that Liz and Sue deal with and try to identify the phrases they use when winding up a call. With regard to the customers at the counter, could this be another case like my long meetings where a few occasions when there has been a problem have made you believe that it is all the time?'

'It could be, but my diary analysis will not show it, as I didn't make any notes on that. I will keep a note for the next few weeks to see if it really is a problem.'

'Good, then we will sit down together and see if there are any problem areas that you can work on. Now what about your "crimes" Sue?'

'Well, I think that we have sorted out some of the problems at home. I know that the problem is that because I like helping people I offer assistance and they accept. It's my fault, not theirs.'

'I'm not so sure that you are altogether right there,' said John. 'Because you are always so willing and helpful, we all tend to think that you won't mind and that you have time to do things for us. As a result, we all make use of you. I think we all need to be aware that you are just as busy as the rest of us and that we must stop imposing on your good nature. In the various books and notes on time management, people who frequently take up other people's time with things they should be doing themselves or things that are unnecessary are called "time-robbers", "time-stealers" or "time bandits". They may only be dropping in for a two-minute social chat; which can be fine, except you might have other things that you would rather do, and an hour later they are still there. Some customers come into that category also, as Jason has found out.'

ACTION PLAN 16

Think about the people who take up your time at work and at home with their problems and chatter and those who somehow or other get you to do jobs for them. Make a list of them in your action plan in chapter 10 and try to analyse the sort of words that they start with, such as 'have you got a minute?' or 'can you spare a couple of minutes just to do this?'. If you are quite content to continue to help them there is no need to take further action; but if you would like to avoid being caught with them in future, think what your response could be next time they approach you and enter it against their names in your action plan.

'John is right: we do lumber you too often,' said Liz, and the others all agreed with her.

'As that concludes the work on our time diaries it is the end of these sessions, apart from the monitoring progress and reporting back at our staff meetings,' said John.

'On behalf of all of us may I thank you for all your help and the time you have given up for us, John,' said Liz. 'We really do appreciate it.'

'I've enjoyed doing it, and I think that it has helped us all to know more about one another and our aspirations. But for now, let's see if the Falcon is open for business.'

SUMMARY

In this chapter our characters have carried out a more detailed analysis of how they can use their time outside of work, with a view to finding areas where they can make reductions to be able to spend more time on their personal development.

They have recognized that they can only take on additional commitments by substituting them for some of the things that they do at present, as we all have the same number of hours per week.

We have seen how Sue's husband, children and mother were ready to support her as soon as they were given an opportunity.

It seems highly likely that because she wants to look after her home and family she has taken over all of the duties, and as a result has deprived them of the chance to contribute.

Helen has decided to try to become elected to the committee of her ski club, but John has pointed out that this should be because it is something that she really *wants* to do, rather than something she thinks others want her to do.

Our characters have discussed the differences between important tasks and urgent ones, and have been shown a method to help them to prioritize the order in which to do them by plotting on a chart.

The need for discussing issues with those who are affected by our decisions and actions has been illustrated by several different examples from our characters.

The analysis of the 'at work' time has revealed a need to introduce some performance indicators for the counter staff by using average times for the different types of interviews. These will enable them to see how they are performing in comparison with their colleagues. This is important, as one of the most common complaints from workers of all grades is that no one tells them how they are performing.

A number of training needs have also been highlighted by the analysis.

The problem of avoiding or putting off tasks that we do not like doing, which is referred to as procrastination, is examined. Liz has now become aware that it is something that she is prone to do, and that awareness in itself plus the help of her colleagues will help her to overcome it.

Both Sue and Liz have identified that they are carrying the baggage, probably from childhood, of wanting to please by agreeing to take on any additional tasks, even to the point of becoming over-committed.

We have been shown by John how to break down big tasks by 'chunking' rather than trying to find large blocks of time to commit to them.

The subject of delegation has been examined, and a discussion has taken place on the reasons people fail to delegate, the best ways of going about it and its benefits.

A warning has been given with regard to 'time-robbers', who are the people who take up some of your hours in doing jobs that they should really be doing, or merely want to chat for long periods.

The team, as they have now become, have agreed to help one another, and have allocated ten minutes at future staff meetings to discuss their progress.

7

Am I on the Right Track, and How will I Know When I Get There?

So far, in looking at setting goals and developing our action plans we have tended to concentrate on those relating to our careers. We have seen how Liz, Sue, Helen and Jason have all decided that qualifications are essential first steps for them. John is the exception here, because at 52 years old his first career progression must be very limited in an industry that traditionally has a young image, and further qualifications are unlikely to help him, even though he is 8 or 13 years from normal retirement at 60 or 65 years of age.

We know that Liz is 26 years old, is currently studying Spanish at evening classes and is taking the company's NVQ4 course in Management. We also know that she is ambitious and would like a manager's job, but that a move to another part of the country for this would probably cause problems between her and her husband, who needs to stay in the locality for his business.

What we do not know is just how ambitious she is. Will she want to progress to an Area Manager or a General Manager? What hobbies and interests would she like to pursue? Is it her intention to have a family? If so, does she see herself returning to full-time work immediately after maternity leave each time?

It is quite possible for her to do all of these, and it is good to see that some people are able to successfully balance demanding careers, families and their leisure interests. However, it has to be said that the higher you go in a career the greater the demands that are made upon you and the greater the dedication and single-mindedness you require. The last chapter demonstrated the need to balance our time, and how spending more time on one part of our lives means giving up some of the hours we spend on something else.

What we need Liz and the others to do is visualize exactly what they would like their lives to look like or consist of at various future times; and then to write a statement which encapsulates it, as suggested in the section on positive thinking in chapter 3.

For example, in Liz's case, she might already have thoughts in her mind that she wants to be a branch manager within the next two years, have two children before she is 30, and return to work straight away. She sees them moving to a four-bedroom house locally which has a large garden that she can do as a relaxation. The house she sees as being in need of refurbishment when they buy it, so that she and Alan can work on it together to personalize it. Alan's business is operating satisfactorily, so that with their two incomes they can afford to run two cars, take their holidays abroad and entertain the wide circle of friends they have made as a result of their involvement at the tennis club and their charity work. She also sees herself becoming an Area Manager when the children are in their mid-teens; but by doing a large amount of motoring, which she enjoys, they would still be able to live in the same place.

That all sounds like day-dreaming, but success in life is frequently about turning day-dreams into reality. We know that Simon, her Area Manager, already sees her as having the potential to be a Branch Manager, and she is on the company management training programme. Also, it would be reasonable for her to think that Alan's business will pick up when the rest of the building industry does. So these 'day-dreams' are quite realistic.

If we look now at the title of this chapter and relate Liz's vision to it, it seems very straightforward. We may think that of course she will know that she is on the right track when she becomes the branch manager or buys the house she wants, as she has been very specific over the sort of life she wants. Unfortunately life is rarely that simple. Yes, she has been very specific in her thoughts, but they may need to change as and when events overtake them – such as Alan's business going into liquidation, or being sold to prevent it going downhill further. The house she has visualized may be far more expensive than they can ever afford, so perhaps this part of her vision is not realistic. If, as a result, Alan has to go to work as a site manager for a big builder, and they buy a three-bedroom semi instead of the four-bedroom detached house, will she still know that she is on the right track?

If we refer back to the planning process in chapter 3, we will recall that we said that planning is not a straightforward linear process. It is a series of loops which all the time lead us back to our objectives to check whether these are still valid given the changes in personal and work constraints. In Liz's case a major change in Alan's situation might well cause her to rethink the life-style that she has set as her goal.

With regard to the house it could well be that they will have several houses before they can aspire to what she would really like. Also, by revisiting her goals at regular intervals she could well find that she has changed her mind over her housing requirements, and now wants them to build one themselves. In that case they need to find a suitable plot of land.

This brings us to one of the most important reasons for setting goals. Because we are bombarded with so much information from our senses, in terms of all of the things we can see, hear, smell, taste and touch at any one time, we very conveniently switch off to most of it. An example of this is that when we drive to work we are often thinking about other things and cannot even remember the route we have taken on that occasion. However, during that time we might notice certain things if we are particularly interested in them, such as if we pass another car of the same make and colour as our own, or of the sort we would particularly like to buy. If we skim through the local paper, certain items of interest seem to leap out of the page at us. If we plant a tree or shrub in our garden, all of a sudden we are aware of many other gardens with the same plant; or it could be people wearing the same type or colour coat we have just bought. This is because we have registered an interest in these items and our brain is responding to that interest and allowing the information past the 'filters'.

It therefore follows that by setting a goal we are declaring an interest in particular information, such as Liz wanting a particular type of house that needs work doing to it, or a plot of land on which to build. Normally she would not even notice advertisements for plots of land or 'for sale' boards, but as soon as she has identified that she is interested they will come to her attention even if she does not specifically look for them. If someone nearby mentions a subject we are interested in we will usually hear their comments, even if they are not speaking to us and are several yards away in another group. A particular example of this, which we must all have experienced at some time, is when someone across a noisy room happens to mention our name.

If we look back at the sort of statement that Liz might write about her vision for the future, we can see that it covers a number of different areas in which goals need to be set and which will have different time-scales. These areas include her career, where she wants first to be a Branch Manager and later an Area Manager; a family of two children within the next four years; a four-bedroomed detached house with a large garden which she and Alan will need to spend a long time in improving. Alan's building company needs to be turned round so that it makes a healthy profit. Their finances need planning so that they can progress towards taking their holidays abroad and running two cars. On the social side, they want to develop their circle of friends at the tennis club. Finally, they want to become involved in charity work.

Each of these major goals has a number of steps that can be identified as shorter-term goals which lead along the road to the goal achievement. Many are interrelated and most will affect the financial planning. For example, the family goal would involve two periods of maternity leave and the cost of child minders for several years; the house purchase will require financing and so will the refurbishment afterwards; the socializing obviously has a cost. The other major budget item, which we discussed in the last two chapters, is that of time. Will she have enough hours in the week to have the life-style that she visualizes for herself?

Each of the shorter goals need to be set along the road towards the achievement of the longer-term goal. As mentioned in chapter 3, these should then be regarded as 'milestones'. The shorter-term goals may be weekly, monthly or three monthly, depending on the nature of the long-term goal and the activities we have identified as being part of it. The length of these goals may vary according to where we are on our journey at any one time. For example, one of the short-term goals for Sue in terms of her career development might have been to free up the time for her to be able to attend her course at college. The activities involved in this included attending the sessions run by John after work, maintaining her time diary for the two weeks, analysing the diary and finding new ways of covering her work at home.

It therefore allows that at any one time we should be able to see from our action plan of the long-term goal how far we have progressed and what the next milestone will be. Each time we reach a milestone we need to check back to our original objective and take another look at any future actions we have planned, to ensure that both the objective and the planned actions are still relevant, before setting our course for the next milestone. If they are not and we need to change the 'destination' we are aiming for, then we will need to revise all of the milestones or actions we have planned in the light of this change of destination. Furthermore, we will need to see how it impacts on all of the other long-term goals we have been working towards.

It is most important that we keep a note of the shorter-term goals that we have successfully achieved, as these will show us how far we have already gone along the road to that long-term goal and provide us with energy and single-mindedness to keep going. For example, let's say we set a goal for furnishing our first house by making a list of all the major things we want for it. If we simply make out a new list from time to time we will lose sight of the things we have crossed off the old lists as we have bought them. Of course we can see the furniture in our home, but the fact that it is there all of the time stops us from noticing it in particular; whereas seeing it crossed off our list will keep us aware of our success.

Checking our course and our progress may appear easy, but often the tools we are using to make judgements for certain goals are very subjective and are not as accurate as modern maps and compasses. On these occasions we need to find other ways of calculating our position. Many people tend to do this by comparing themselves with the progress of their peers. This can lead to them being demoralized, if they focus on one or two outstanding successes; or becoming complacent, if they choose to compare their progress with those who have not done so well. Such comparisons are flawed by the fact that we rarely know what the actual ambitions and goals of others are. The reasons for this are many, but the chief ones include the fact that few people set goals for themselves in the structured way that we are recommending, and the ambitions and aspirations that they declare to others may not be the ones that they really want. We had an example of this in chapter 2, when John felt that he had to answer the question of where he wanted to be in five years' time by saying that he wanted more responsibility – when he would really have liked early retirement.

If the shorter or smaller goals we have set ourselves are clear and measurable they will indeed act as milestones on our journey. However, there could, for example, be a long wait between one promotion and the next, and we would need to know whether we are still on the right path. Sometimes this can come from feedback at our annual or six-monthly appraisal interview. However, this so-called 'feedback' is often given in very glowing terms to make us feel good and to allow the interviewer to have an easy interview; and criticisms, whether justified or not, go unstated. Ideally we need someone more senior than us in our company or organization who will act as our adviser, counsellor and role model, and this someone we refer to as a *mentor*.

Some companies have formal mentor schemes, where senior managers volunteer to act as mentors for management trainees, graduate recruits, junior managers and staff members with promotion potential. The success of this very much depends on the individuals concerned and what agendas they are working to. Such formal schemes, whilst assisting the junior manager, will be heavily weighted with the interests of the company and organization; and the best interests of the individual and the company may not necessarily be the same. However, mentors appointed for a specific short-term purpose, such as whilst the more junior person is undertaking training or is starting in a new role, can be very successful.

The best results come from a less formal relationship, that starts as a result of a senior manager and a junior manager/staff member working well together and developing a respect for one another's abilities, knowledge or potential. The junior manager/ staff member then needs to feel able to ask the senior manger whether they will act as mentor for them. In some cases this will simply evolve. It is, however, better that it is discussed openly, so that the junior member is not seen by others to be ingratiating themselves with the more senior manager. The relationship between the mentor and the junior manager/staff member should be a two-way one, with the junior person feeling able to pass information to the mentor so that they can discuss problems jointly.

In our case study we can see that Simon could be the mentor for Liz. He is not her immediate line manager and has already shown an interest in her progress and future. However, we know that his view of her future would include her having to move to another part of the country to take a manager's job, and this would cause problems in her marriage because of her husband's business. In this case she will need to discuss at least her career goals with Simon, so that he does not recommend her for a manager's job elsewhere. Obviously if he recommended her for a promotion and she then turned it down she would have caused him embarrassment and would lose his support – or worse, would have alienated him. She needs to ensure that she also discusses her career with her line manager, John. They started to get on better in the last chapter, and if he knows what her plans are then he may be less suspicious and antagonistic towards her. He may even be helpful.

Also in our case study we can see that John could be the mentor for Helen. She normally reports to Liz as her immediate line manager, but is going to work closely with John on the business development project. He has already arranged with the area manager for some training and development for her, and in chapter 5 volunteered to help her with her time management. She is only three years older than his daughter, and guiding an 'adopted' child in his or her career is quite a common activity for managers of many years' experience. However, it will be necessary for her to let Liz know what is happening so that she does not feel that her position as Helen's line manager is being undermined, just as John obviously feels over the interest Simon shows in Liz's career. Also, she will need to be careful that she does not take on John's jaundiced view of the company resulting from his bitterness over the takeover.

We can see from these two examples that whilst Liz will have her appraisal interviews with John she will also have informal career discussions with Simon. This way she will receive different views of her progress towards her career goals. Similarly, Helen, and possibly Sue and Jason also, can make use of John as their mentor and Liz as their line manager. This will give them a more balanced view of their progress than simply relying on their own opinions, which can vary between elation and despair, according to how they are feeling.

THINK POINT

Consider who could act as mentor for you in your career. Who would you really respect as a counsellor, advisor and role model? How can you arrange for them to fulfil the role for you? (Enter your answers in your Action Plan.)

The opinion of peers, family and friends can be used, but caution is necessary here. In our travel agency Helen, Sue and Jason are all looking to progress via qualifications, so there is some common ground here. However, Helen is going to follow a different route from Sue and Jason, which means that they are not really in a position to give an informed opinion over the route she is taking and vice versa. The real danger can come from those so-called friends, peers and family members who are not ambitious and do not see why you should be different from them. In this case they will actively discourage you from progressing to keep you at their level, rather than be shown up by you. Some partners may want from a personal ego point of view to be the successful one in the relationship.

An example of this could be Liz's husband Alan, who only seems to be seeing things from his point of view. His vision of the future could be that his business is doing well, they have two children, they live in a four-bedroom detached house. Liz is content to stay at home looking after the house and garden, and spending time at the tennis club, where she is the secretary and doing charity work. As she gave up work when they had a family she looks after all of his company books for him. If this is Alan's vision or agenda, which is very much based on his own achievements, he is not going to be any support to Liz in her career and could easily hold her back. It therefore follows that his opinion of whether she is on the right track or not and how far she has progressed will be worthless to her. On the other hand, Sue's husband Tony is actively supporting her in her ambitions and is being very helpful so that she can attend her course. He is already seeing the benefits of her working in that they are having a family holiday in the USA.

THINK POINT

How does your vision of what you want for the future mesh with that of your partner? Do you really know what each of you wants, or have you not discussed with them? Have any peers, family and/or friends tried to discourage you and persuade you to abandon or lower your aspirations? Whose opinions do you need to avoid asking in future?

Besides being held back by the declared views of friends, colleagues and family we can also be held back by ourselves as a result of our desire to 'belong' or 'fit in'. Our efforts to be considered one of the boys or girls can make it more difficult for those above us to visualize us in a managerial position. The image we create is therefore very important if we really want to get promoted. We need to look at the way in which we dress when we go to work and whilst we are at work. Is our hair-style appropriate for an aspiring manager? Will our behaviour, attitudes and the opinions we express make it more difficult for us to be seen as managerial potential? Conformance in our dress and behaviour does not mean becoming a different person, as our personalities are much stronger than these outward signs, which could be left over, as baggage, from our more rebellious youth. When and if we are promoted, we would need to change so that we again 'belong' to the new group we have just joined. It therefore follows that if we enhance our prospects by modifying our dress and behaviour now then it is sensible to do so. There may be changes that we have to make, but these are part of the price of wanting to get on, in the same way as giving up doing something we like so that we can attend a course at college. If we want something enough then we will be willing to pay the price.

THINK POINT

Make a note of the sort of clothes you wear for work and alongside it make another list of the clothes your boss or the manager you most respect wears. Analyse the differences and try to work out why you choose the clothes that you wear for work. Also, have a look at your hair-style: is it more appropriate for work or for going out on a Saturday night?

So far in this chapter we have only looked at the people who are still near to the beginning of their careers, and who are therefore making plans and setting goals that will very much affect the majority of their careers and how far they are likely to progress. However, we are all capable of growing and developing in countless number of ways for the remainder of our lives, or until our brains are no longer functioning properly. We can continue to set goals for the whole of this period in order to extract the most we can from our relatively short lives. Examples to us all here include the recent story of the 106-year-old person who has enrolled for a college course, and the growing number of pensioners each year who complete the annual marathon races in London, New York and Sydney, or who take university degrees.

If we look at the case of John we know that he has said to Eileen, his wife, that he would like to take early retirement in, say, five years' time, and then to have a part-time job. Early retirement would of course enable him to give more time to the things that he really wants to do, such as his golf and magistrate's work. He also sees them eventually moving to a bungalow on the south coast, where no doubt he will still expect to play golf and do his garden. How much of this is to do with his comfort zones that we mentioned in chapter 2? We know that he was moved out of his comfort zone at work when the company was taken over and his status was reduced. Since then he has set his goals outside of work, and in chapter 5 we recall that he mentioned goals in connection with his golf and in reading classical literature. However, he appears to be becoming enthusiastic over the new campaign that Simon has asked him to do, and relations with

Simon and Liz are improving. He is also feeling more accepted and needed by his junior staff as a result of the time management sessions and his interest in their development. All of this may mean that he has found a new challenge and is re-energized in terms of work.

If we look at what we know of his vision, once again we are faced with the question of whether it fits in with what his wife wants. Moving from one part of the country to another very much affects comfort zones, as it involves the loss of so many of the familiar things from everyday life. Eileen would find herself having to make new friends, use new shops, find out where all the local amenities are, sort out a new house and garden, and so forth. It might also mean them moving away from their children and relations, as well as friends and acquaintances. Although John mentioned to Eileen that he would like to take early retirement in five years' time, have they discussed his vision of the future or has Eileen kept quiet about what she wants, thinking that there is plenty of time?

In her book *Fine Tune Your Brain*, Genie Laborde uses the expression 'dovetailing' to describe the process by which two people discuss the outcomes that they want and by their communication and negotiation are able to fit them together to form a really strong joint. In this way if John and Eileen have fully discussed and agreed on the future life that they want together, they will both be using their energies towards a common goal and be able to plan for it. Unfortunately their time-scales will be affected by the uncertainty of whether John will get early retirement or not. However, they know when he is officially due to retire and can start planning for that when it is nearer the time. It simply means that if he is able to leave earlier they would be able to bring their plans forward.

But it must be emphasized that retirement should never be seen as the end of our working lives; it merely indicates the need for different goals and new uses for some of our 168 hours per week. It is also too early for John, who still has either eight or thirteen years before his official retirement, to be thinking about such things. He very much needs to be setting important goals that can be worked on now and for at least the next five years.

We have all come across people who suffer from the *'when then'* syndrome. They can be identified by their comments such as *'when* I retire, *then* I am going to . . .', or *'when* the children leave home, *then* I will . . .'. The sad thing about these people is that even when the event they are waiting for arrives, they seldom do what they said they would. If John belonged to this group he would be sitting around looking miserable whilst waiting for eight to thirteen years for retirement – and just think what percentage of his life that represents. Obviously he would be hoping for early retirement, which would reduce the period, but the more time that went by without this happening the more miserable and bitter he could become. This in turn would sour his home life and the atmosphere at work, and he would become someone that people would start to avoid. Fortunately we know that although John has said that he would like early retirement he lives a full life and continues to set himself goals.

THINK POINT

Are there any 'when thens' in your life? If there are, what goals have you set for them, what plans have you made, and what action have you taken?

SUMMARY

This chapter has looked at how we might set short- and long-term personal goals, and how we can measure our progress towards those goals.

Consideration has been given to those towards the end of their careers as well as to those just beginning work.

The importance of colleagues, especially those willing to act as mentors, was considered. The chapter concluded with an indication of those things that can stand in the way of our achieving the goals we have set for ourselves.

8
Where do I Go from Here?

In chapter 2 we talked about 'comfort zones' and about how people cling to what they know and understand. Resistance to change is very common, and many books have been written on how to overcome it. We also looked at the need to carry out an environmental analysis (PEST analysis) both from the organizational point of view (*In Charge, Managing Operations*) and from the individual's (chapter 2 of this volume). For whether we like it or not the world is an ever-changing place.

Nothing ever remains the same.

The world you woke up to this morning is very different to the one in which you went to sleep last night. And the world you come home to this evening will have changed even more.

Unless we understand this fundamental point we will all eventually be left behind by events, wondering what went wrong.

THINK POINT

Listen to the news on television this evening and make a note of the headlines. Listen again next morning and make a note of the headlines now. What changes have occurred?

At the beginning of this volume you were introduced to the BACK analysis. Now we are going to look at the FRONT analysis.

FRONT stands for:

be **F**orward looking
Review progress
be **O**pen with those closest to you
adopt **N**ew plans where appropriate
Take opportunities when they come up

Let's look at these in a little more detail.

FORWARD LOOKING

If we do not continue to look forward we won't be able to make plans. In chapter 7 we looked at some of the aspirations Liz or her husband Alan might have. If we have no personal objectives we will drift aimlessly through life. Worse, we may well accidentally stumble upon an objective after earlier turning down an opportunity to develop the skills, knowledge or material possessions that would enable us to achieve it.

The only certain thing is that things will change. We need to keep abreast of what those changes will be and of how they might affect us. Being proactive in this way, it is more likely that you will be ready for change when it comes.

A good example of this is planning for retirement. Many people arrive at the day without really giving it any thought. Suddenly there is a great void in their life where work used to be. Often they become depressed and unable to cope. Those people who plan ahead for it usually have a very clear idea of how they intend to spend their increased leisure time, by taking up new hobbies or interests (or becoming even more involved in current ones), or by travelling more, or in some cases by taking on less stressful part-time work.

THINK POINT

Are there any planned fundamental changes that are about to occur in your life, such as changing job, being offered a promotion or starting a family, for example?

REVIEWING

It is necessary to review our progress at intervals to make sure that either:

We are making progress towards where we want to be

or

We are *adopting* our life objectives in accordance with our changing beliefs or attitudes.

It is a fact that our attitudes and beliefs may well change as we get older. Many people who enjoyed pop music in their early years find that they are more comfortable listening to opera in later life. Similarly, many who would be considered nonconformists or rebels in their youth settle down to become pillars of the establishment in later years.

One idea is to carry out a major review of what you have done and achieved on New Year's Eve every year over a glass of wine or beer. This is probably best done at the beginning of the evening! You could follow this by updating your aspirations and life objectives on New Year's morning.

This would be the equivalent of your appraisal interview at work, but you would discuss things with your partner (or carry out a self-analysis) rather than with your boss.

Just as at work you would expect to review your performance on a less formal basis at intervals throughout the year, so you can review your progress every few months.

In the review it is important to consider whether you have:

- done the things you wanted to in the year
- gained the skills and knowledge that you intended
- changed your aspirations
- identified any new skills that are needed
- changed your attitudes or beliefs

THINK POINT

Now try to identify three things, either at work or at home, that you have achieved during the past twelve months.

BE OPEN

As we have seen throughout this volume, it is very easy to hide what you really feel from other people. Sometimes even from yourself!

We have also seen that it is vital that you gain support from those around you, both at work and at home. Liz and Alan are very good examples here. They both have fears for the future about where their respective careers may lead them and the effect that might have upon their marriage. As yet, however, these fears have not been shared openly, and their suppression is building up a store of possible trouble in the future.

NEW PLANS

As mentioned above, the world is ever changing and it will be necessary to adapt your objectives both at work and at home to the new situations that arise. This really is a state of mind. Some people can see very quickly what they need to do in a new situation. Others complain about it and rail about why it has happened.

Being aware of the inevitability of change brings one very great advantage. It makes you appreciate things more because you know that they will change. For example, if you have currently got the best boss at work that you have ever had, you will appreciate it even more if you understand that it is very likely that soon one or other of you is likely to move on either for promotion or development. It is likely to heighten your enjoyment of a favourable situation. It also make you less likely to waste this time in negative activities such as conflict.

The same applies in an unfavourable situation, as you can console yourself that it may not last for ever.

TAKE YOUR OPPORTUNITIES

We have all heard people who have said:

'Well I could have done that if I had wanted to but ...

I preferred to do something else
I didn't want to move house
I had the children to look after
My husband/wife didn't feel that I should risk it
I already had a good job'

You may have heard one or two others! In many cases there are genuine reasons. In some cases they seemed important at the time. In others they may well have been a way of avoiding the challenge.

After all, if you don't try something you can't fail at it. Better still, you can go through life claiming that if you had tried it you would have been good at it. By passing over the opportunity of, say, a promotion at work, there is no risk of failure.

Indeed, if the other person who did take the opportunity is successful then you can bask in the glory of the success that would obviously have been yours ... if you had wanted it.

We all surround ourselves with limiting factors like the ones above. What we need to be sure of is that they really are limiting factors and not just excuses.

For example:

Many people DO move house
Many people employ child minders (or relatives)
Some organizations have crèche facilities
Some people DO give up jobs they enjoy to take on greater challenges

We need to ask ourselves why we are not prepared to break out from these limiting factors. If the answer is that our current values are such that any of these factors would lead to a reduction in our quality of life and our satisfaction levels, then we are probably right to accept them as limiting.

We may feel that it is very important that our children have a significant amount of contact with parents, and that this would not be possible with both of them out at work.

Or we may feel that it is important to be near aged and ailing relatives, so a house move could not be considered.

On the other hand, we also know that nothing ever remains the same, and we do need to take advantage of those opportunities that may help us to achieve our aspirations. Once an opportunity has gone it may never reappear. The next opportunity may fall to someone else . . .

We may be left with that awful feeling of: If only . . .

THINK POINT

Try to think back to the last time you said 'If only . . .' What were the limiting factors that prevented you from grasping the opportunity? Do they still apply now?

Let's now ask each of our main characters in turn to carry out a FRONT analysis.

John is feeling pretty good at the moment. Let's hear what he has to say.

'Well, I've certainly learned a lot these last few months. The first thing that I've realized is that there is a lot more to look forward to than I thought. I had really considered that these next few years before retirement would be a sort of limbo, with me just going through the motions and turning up for work each day.

However, this new project that Simon has given me is really interesting. It's getting me involved in all sorts of areas that are new to me. I hadn't really thought that business travel would be that interesting, and that's why I had never really got too involved before. But I've had my eyes opened. I'm meeting some very sharp and stimulating people. Some of them have even come for a round of golf with me, and one particular acquaintance is fast becoming a personal friend. In fact he and his wife are coming round to dinner next week.

The campaign is going very well. We are meeting all the targets that Simon set, and I must say that Helen has been a great help. She is very enthusiastic and has thrown herself wholeheartedly into the project.

It's not only Helen who I enjoy working with, but all of the rest of the team too, since we carried out the time management sessions. We all seem to be working more as a team now. I can even get on with Liz. I can see now that she has her own problems and is tackling them in the best way she can.

I've learned a lot more about myself recently as well as about others. I've begun to share my hopes and fears more with Eileen. She's taking a much more positive attitude too. We sat down the other night and decided what we wanted out of the rest of our lives.

What we really want is to see the children settled into careers, and work at something that we are really interested in until we retire. Eileen has begun a part-time job as a personal assistant in a local firm. I met her boss while playing golf and during the conversation we realized that he was looking for someone he could trust to do a good job, and Eileen was looking for something local and interesting.

Yes, identifying who can help you along the road is certainly important. I won't forget that lesson in a long time!

And as for that bungalow on the south coast. Well, we've decided to stay here where we know people rather than have to start afresh when we get there. It was only something to look forward to really. Now we've got quite a lot to look forward to here. Mind you, we'll keep an open mind. If we win the lottery, who knows what plans we'll make.

The main thing is that my attitude has changed. I was content to mope around and blame life and the universe for the situation we were in. I had a boring job and Eileen had none at all!

However, I feel that we've begun to make things happen for ourselves. We've been given a couple of opportunities and we're taking them. We haven't been so happy for some time. We're going to have a holiday this year to celebrate. We may go on a cruise . . .

We've set ourselves some objectives for the next year:

to enjoy a holiday
to continue to make new friends;
to reduce my handicap at golf to 10;
to help Samantha start a career when she leaves university this
    year;
at work, to try and encourage Jason and help him to become
    more involved.

I'm also going to talk to Simon about future opportunities.'

John left the room humming his favourite tune. When we first met him he was depressed, going nowhere and achieving little.

Now all that has changed because he has taken control of his life again.

Let's catch up with Liz. She has a very pensive look.

'Oh, my job's going very well. Simon was very pleased with that report. A lot of my problems of time management have been sorted out and I've even begun to delegate more. This means that I'm not staying late at the office so often and now rarely take work home. This has made things a lot easier with Alan and I'm beginning to enjoy my home life a lot more.

Even John seems to be much more pleasant than ever before. I enjoy the work and Simon has been hinting about greater things in store so there could be a promotion in the offing soon.

And that's the problem.

I realize now that although I have thought about where Alan and I might be going over the next few years, I have never really stopped to think how we're going to get there. I have this vague idea of what we'll be doing and that I'll have a better job and we'll have a better house, but when I really sit down and try to visualize how we can achieve those things there's just one big blank.

We have both concentrated on the present and just assumed that the future would turn out right. I think we've both just ignored it because it would force us to face up to some pretty important questions.

Now, if you asked me where I see us in five years' time, I don't find the question so easy to answer. I can't really picture myself still working at this branch because I would hope to have moved on. But where to?

I think I can picture Alan still running the business, but that may well be simply because I can't see him doing anything else. We've never thought about it.

I'm currently doing various courses with a view to getting on in my career, but I have absolutely no idea of what the next big step will be.

I haven't really sat down and considered my options. I might have to move for a promotion within this company, but there are other travel agents in the area. Who says that I couldn't do just as well with them and stay in the area? Certainly the qualifications that I am working towards are likely to make me even more marketable than I am at present. The skills I am developing while

I am working on the course and in my current job will also help me to move on if I decide to do so.

I've also been thinking more about whether I would like to have a family. I'm not getting any younger! The later I leave it the harder it will be to interrupt my career. Alan and I haven't even spoken about this for a long time, so I don't know how he feels about it.

I was talking to Claire, Helen's best friend, the other day, and she was telling me about the number of people in her company who are now working from home. When I think about it I could do quite a lot of my job from home. I don't really need to be in the office all day, especially with the communication equipment that is available today. Perhaps the company would consider giving me a computer and I could spend less time travelling. That would be ideal, especially if I had to go further afield for a promotion. It might mean that I would only have to travel on perhaps two or three days a week instead of every day, or instead of having to move.

There's even the possibility that I could go freelance and work for several local companies doing the things that I am good at and that I enjoy doing. That way I could use my home as a base and I would have even less travel. And I would see more of Alan. It would be a major step but it is an option, and if I succeeded it would give me back a large degree of control of my life that I seem to have lost recently.

The more I think about things the more obvious it becomes that Alan and I haven't been communicating too well recently. I think the time has come for us to be much more open and honest with each other about what we want from life. I'm going to suggest that we have a long talk about it this evening.

It's important that we think this through or we may spend the rest of our lives saying "if only . . .".'

Meanwhile, in Simon's office a letter was lying in his in tray. He has been offered the post of Regional Manager. This is what he has been waiting for. His salary will increase considerably and he will be allocated a top-of-the-range car. He is feeling elated, excited, anxious.

What if he fails? After all, he is not yet 36 and is relatively inexperienced. He spent a very short time as an Area Manager.

This mixture of thoughts at such a time is not unusual. We have all experienced excitement at being offered an opportunity, and then suddenly felt worried that we might not be able to live up to it.

It is at this stage that Simon needs to stop and think about what he needs to do to give himself the best opportunity for success. The first thing he needs to do is to consider the skills that he will need in his new job. He then needs to carry out an audit of his own strengths and weaknesses and identify where he needs to improve. Yes, this would be a good time to carry out a personal SWOT analysis.

He has been concentrating on developing a much more participative style of management recently. It worked very well with John, and he also used it to good effect on several other occasions.

He therefore needs to consider who can help him to be successful, and he has already given some thought to that. There is a letter in his out tray addressed to Liz.

Jason is a young man at the beginning of his career. In fact, we know that it is only very recently that he thought about his job as a career. Now that he is engaged to Paula he has had to give more serious thought to his and their future.

He has begun to manage his time more effectively and has pulled out of some of the tasks he carried out for the football club. However, as he sits at his desk he reflects on what the future holds: he tries to look forward and sees him and Paula getting married and buying a house. Then . . . nothing. He hasn't really looked beyond that stage.

'I'm really horrified that I seem to have no vision of where I'm going after Paula and I are married. It just seems to be a large void. Oh yes, I can fill it with a couple of children and a nice house and perhaps a better job, but they are *other people's* visions rather than mine. They are what you see people doing on TV or what you saw your parents doing. I have to try to look ahead at what I want and what *we* want.'

Jason has carried out the first stage of a FRONT analysis and he does not like what he sees. He resolves to give it some thought.

He decides to review what he has done so far.

'Well, I'm very well thought of at the football club and I do play very well. However, it is unlikely that I'm going to be snapped up by a professional club, so this part of my life is likely to be recreational, and I'm not going to make any money at it.

That being the case, I do need a career. I have a very good job at the moment, though it is a bit boring and repetitive. I think I'm capable of more demanding work. After all, I am studying for a qualification now, and I feel I know a lot more about the business than when I started. John has said that he would try to help me and I think I know just the way he can do it. I'll ask him if he has any special projects that I can do. I think I'll also ask Liz if she can delegate some of her work to me. I wonder if she would be prepared to share out some of my most routine work so that everyone gets a little bit, rather than me being stuck with it all. I'll tell her how I feel. I'm sure she'll understand.

I'm going to work hard at this job. I'll show everyone that I am worth promoting when the opportunity comes along.'

Jason has moved through the next two stages of the FRONT analysis. He is going to be open about how he feels and has adopted a new strategy.

He has also taken at least one opportunity by enrolling on his course. He is already aware of the new skills he is developing and these should stand him in good stead. Perhaps other opportunities will follow . . .

Helen and Sue were the last to leave the office and decided to pop into the Falcon on their way home.

'You know, a few weeks ago I wouldn't have had time to do this,' said Sue. 'Not only that, I wouldn't have done it even if I had the time, because it is something for *me* and I would have given that a very low priority. I would have rushed home and started to do things like tidying up or putting the dinner on. Now I try to do something for *me* every day, even if it's only a little thing like popping in for a quick drink with you on the way home.'

'Yes, I've taken a good hard look at myself recently and I'm doing a lot of things differently now,' said Helen. For one thing, I have set myself some goals. I realize that I've rather been drifting through the last few years. I want to make sure that the next few years really count. I've made a conscious decision to get involved in the things I enjoy rather than standing by and watching others do them.'

THINK POINT

Look back over the last seven days. Itemize something that you did for *you* on each day, such as reading, pursuing a hobby, watching a favourite television programme. Only list those things that you deliberately set out to do. If you haven't done at least one thing for *you* on most of those days, you may need to ask yourself some questions about your quality of life. Are you running your life or is it running you?

'For example, I am definitely going to take on the development course. That's a work/career goal. But I've also realized that one of my favourite things on TV is to watch winter sports such as ice skating and skiing. Up to now that's all I have done, watch, but I'm determined to change things. When I think of all the thousands of people who take part in these sports while I sit at home and watch them, it makes me feel furious at my own lethargy. If they can skate and ski, then so can I. I was very impressed listening to Jason, who although he had over-committed himself, was still enjoying being involved in his favourite sport.

I've got tomorrow morning off and I'm going to the skating rink to give it a try. I've also brought a whole lot of brochures home with me. I've always wanted to go on a skiing holiday and now I'm going to do it. I have some money saved up for a holiday, so I don't really know what was stopping me. I think I felt it was all too much effort, or perhaps that I wouldn't be able to do it.'

Helen has realized what many people fail to realize. We don't have to stand around and watch other people do enjoyable and interesting things. We can get involved ourselves. How many people watch motor racing on TV, but have never actually attended a live event and felt the excitement at first hand? How many people love to watch cricket, but have never even considered joining their local village team; or if they are unable to play, at least got involved in some other way?

How many TV gardeners wonder at the great ideas they see but 'never have the time or energy' to put them into practice in their own garden?

When did you last go to a concert instead of listening to the record at home?

The important thing about doing things, or at least attending events first hand, is that you are likely to meet interesting people, perhaps discover new friends, but even more importantly, you will create a life full of memories and experiences that you can recall and build upon in later life.

In many activities there are three types of people:

The doers – those who actually perform the activity;
The supporters – those who are present during the activity and become involved in some way or other;
The passives – those who are content to confine their enjoyment to remote spectating via TV or newspaper.

People who *do* things tend to be interesting to be with and to talk to. Supporters may enjoy a particular activity but may not have the aptitude or physical ability to take part. They will be present at some stage of the activity and are likely to be involved in the experience and the atmosphere. Passive people view the event at third or fourth hand. They miss many of the vital and stimulating parts of the activity.

THINK POINT

Consider four activities that you enjoy. How would you describe yourself in each: doer, supporter, or passive?

Of course we can't all be doers in every activity that we enjoy. But if you find that you have rated yourself as a passive in all four of the activities you have identified, you might ask yourself whether you are taking advantage of all your opportunities.

In many cases we are either supporters or passives when we would really like to be doers; or passives when we would like to be supporters. We need to ask ourselves what is preventing us. It might be:

- lack of time
- lack of money or equipment
- lack of skill or ability
- physical or mental disability
- lack of confidence
- lack of energy
- fear of failing

Or any number of reasons. The important thing is that if you find yourself being passive when you would rather be a doer or a supporter you need to try to identify the real thing that is preventing you from achieving it. Once you have done so you may be able to overcome it.

The main point to remember is that many people who are doers have overcome enormous obstacles to take part in something that they enjoy.

You might be able to overcome yours.

'Well,' said Sue, 'You certainly are taking a really positive attitude. I'm going to give what you've just said some serious thought. I've always thought that there were things I'd like to do but just assumed that I couldn't do them for one reason or another. I'm going to find out what's stopping me. Thanks, Helen.'

We've listened to our main characters and all of them seem to have carried out at least some parts of the FRONT analysis.

We know where each individual wants to go, but before we leave our travel agency let's consider the organization. What advantages are there to be gained for the agency now that its employees are managing themselves in a more positive way?

After all, the business was going quite well when we first arrived at the beginning of the book!

Well, on the face of it the business was doing well, but there was a lot going on (or not going on when it should have been) beneath the surface, which could have boiled over at any time. There was, for example, quite a lot of stress.

In chapter 4 we identified Helen, John and Liz as suffering from various degrees of stress. All of them seem to have worked their way through the problems, except perhaps Liz, who at least has resolved to talk things through with Alan. She has made a major step forward here.

True, the organization may lose her to a rival firm, but if they try to help her resolve her problem in a positive way – such as offering her a position nearer home, allowing her to be flexible in her hours so she can commute, or letting her do some work from home, for example – they may well reap great benefits from the additional loyalty that is likely to ensue. Even if they do lose her they will at least lose the stress that would inevitably follow from the unresolved situation.

John has found new confidence and Helen now has some direction to her life.

This reduction in stress will bring benefits in that problems that could have arisen are much less likely to arise now.

There were also clearly a lot of problems with the management of time. Each individual has developed a range of strategies for dealing with this, and the agency will reap the benefits.

Most of our characters are also determined to alter the balance of their lives so that they do more of the things they enjoy. This is likely to allow them to develop a number of new skills, and their energy levels may well rise again, bringing major benefits to the organization.

All of the individuals now have a clearer idea of where they are going in life and what they want out of it and, in particular, from their careers. They all seem to be much more motivated. Several are committed to gaining relevant work-based qualifications that are likely to move the organization's skills level up a notch.

So the organization is likely to gain a lot from allowing and encouraging individuals to develop themselves. It is important that it continues to offer support to them so that they can build upon the foundation that has been laid.

Let's come back and visit in a couple of year's time and see what actually does happen . . .

ACTION PLAN 17

Now turn to chapter 10 and fill in a FRONT analysis in your Action Plan.

Earlier, in chapter 2, we introduced you to the Belbin team roles and asked you to form an opinion of which team type characteristics the main characters of this book were displaying. You may well have drawn the following conclusions:

Simon displays the characteristics of a *shaper*. He is dynamic and challenging. His subordinates, such as John and Liz, appear to be rather in awe of him, and we may assume that he can be blunt and to the point when necessary.

John shows the typical characteristics of an *implementer*, especially in chapter 4, when he sets about turning Simon's idea for a new business campaign into a real plan. He also shows a lack of flexibility at first in his reaction to Helen.

John also shows that he could be a *co-ordinator* too, which you might expect from his position in the company. However, he shows little of this in chapter 4. It is only in chapters 5 and 6, when he is developing his time management programme (another example of his *implementer* characteristics), that he really shows his aptitude for drawing out contributions from the team.

Indeed, it is apparent in chapter 4 that the team is not working very well together and are tending to pull in different directions. Only in chapters 5 and 6 do we see them develop, largely thanks to John, into a working team.

Liz appears to be a *resource investigator*. She rises enthusiastically to the new challenge but can soon become bored, as we saw with her report for Simon in chapters 4 and 5. She also appeared to be rather afraid of delegating and may well be showing the allowable weakness of the *completer finisher*.

Sue is clearly a *teamworker*. Most of her efforts both at work – when she approached John on Helen's behalf in chapter 4 and at home where we saw in chapter 5 that she makes sure that the rest of the family is happy before doing anything for herself – are oriented on others.

Jason appears to be a *completer finisher*. He holds so many offices at the football club that it may well be that he is afraid to let anyone else do them in case they make a mess of them. He also appears to show the allowable weakness in being rather hesitant and nervous on the telephone with customers, especially when they seem to have a problem.

Helen appears to be a *teamworker* in that she prefers everything to be going along without conflict. She may also lack the ability to make crunch decisions, which may have been holding her back from deciding upon her own career. She may also be a *resource investigator* because she, like Liz, tends to lose interest easily when the newness of the project has worn off.

Most of the team members are likely to be specialists to some degree.

The team does appear to lack two essential roles:

Plant
Monitor Evaluator

If this is so, then the team is likely to be rather lacking in new ideas, though it may well be that Simon is able to provide in this area. The new business promotion idea may well bear this out.

There does not, however, appear to be anyone who displays clearly the characteristics of a *monitor evaluator*. This could well mean that the team could follow the wrong course of action and be well down the road before it realizes that it has gone wrong.

Perhaps if they expand the team in future they should give consideration to bringing someone into it who displays the *monitor evaluator* characteristics. They would then appear to have the basis of a very successful team according to Belbin.

SUMMARY

In this chapter we have looked at the importance of:

looking forward and having some direction to follow

carrying out regular reviews of where we are
communicating openly and honestly with those nearest to us
being aware of new strategies that may become available
taking opportunities
making time for doing the things *you* want
taking an active part in activities that you enjoy
individual development to the organization as a whole

9
Personal Competence in Action

EMIRATES, BRITISH AIRWAYS AND PRINCESS CRUISES

Given that the scenario around which this volume has been written has been set in a travel agent, it seems appropriate to look at examples of organizational excellence and the difference personal competence can make to the product from within the travel industry.

Emirates, British Airways and Princess Cruises all fit this model of excellence: they provide consistent service and quality at a price that makes them accessible to a large number of people, and they do it through the attitudes and the competence of their people. They are not alone in offering an excellent product, and they have been chosen to serve as representatives of excellence within the industry, not as the sole suppliers of high service standards.

EMIRATES

Emirates, the airline of the United Arab Emirates, operate a fleet of predominantly Airbus Industrie aircraft, and serve Europe, the Middle East and Asia from a small state in the Arabian Gulf. Only formed in 1985, they have already won awards for service, including the prestigious 'Airline of the Year 1994' awarded by

Executive Travel and *Wagon Lit*. In the opinion of the authors, their economy-class service is as good as business class on many larger airlines. True, they only have a small fleet and the route network cannot be compared to the large airlines, who have to provide a consistent service over many more daily flights. But as a model for excellence they take some beating. Their staff are well trained and well looked after, with housing being arranged and so on. Those staff are what makes the experience excellent and not just acceptable, and this is the key point about excellence – excellence is a product of *personal competence*.

The Emirates fleet is relatively new and a great deal of care has gone into the physical layout of the aircraft. As mentioned above, even economy-class passengers have a six-channel seat-back video and a footrest. The aircraft interiors are decorated in a light and airy paint scheme, and there is an in-flight information system via central television schemes that gives a map representation of the aircraft position and data regarding progress. Cultural sensitivities are not forgotten: announcements are in Arabic and English and there is a regular display via the flight information system of the direction and distance to Mecca. Food and drink are excellent – parts of the menu were developed under the direction of Emirate's guest chef, Mr Bernard Gaume, of the London Hyatt Carlton Tower Hotel. Mr Gaume was the 1992 Catey Awards 'Chef of the Year'.

Emirates are a good example of how the mix of physical and human resources has been managed to produce an excellent product that has not been diluted through growth. The airline was formed because the government in Dubai were concerned that the regional carriers in the area were not providing Dubai with an effective service. Dubai already possessed an aircraft infrastructure via the DNATA, which provided both reservations and ticketing, engineering and in-flight services to airlines serving Dubai. From 8 aircraft in 1991 the fleet grew to 18 in 1994, with a planned expansion to 30. This will transform Emirates from an Arabian Gulf-based carrier serving international destinations, to an international airline with its main hub in Dubai. Destinations already stretch from Manchester in the UK to Manilla in the Philippines, with a series of regional routes in the Middle East. Thirty-four separate destinations were served in 1994. In 1994 the airline carried in excess of 2 million passengers and received the 'Airline of the Year' award, together with awards for 'Best Long Haul Carrier', 'Best In-flight Food and Drink', 'Best In-flight Entertainment' and 'Best Carrier to the Middle East'. With the introduction of the Boeing 777 in the late 1990s, Emirates will have the option of flying direct to the USA. Transfers at the hub in Dubai are quick and efficient and the airport itself is modern and spacious. Whilst these physical resources are excellent, without dedicated and well-trained staff they would be as nothing.

Cabin crew comprise 42 nationalities with an average age of 24. Given the strategic plans of the airline, they are 'growing their own' cabin crew so that the expansion will be resourced using people who understand the culture and values of the airline. Understanding culture and applying that knowledge to the improvement of service and product is a feature of personal competence.

Given the importance of people in a service environment, it is no coincidence that training and care of staff form important parts of the airline's philosophy. Accommodation in Dubai is provided for cabin crew. The training programme for staff not only covers operational, functional and safety aspects, but there is a strong emphasis on supervision and management. Emirates training department has recently been recognized as a National Examinations Board for Supervisory Management (NEBSM) 'Centre of Excellence' for their work at supervisory/front-line management training throughout the organization – the very level which the *In Charge* series supports.

THINK POINT

Emirates are expanding. What problems, relating to standards of service and product, could this cause? If your organization is either expanding or contracting, what issues is this bringing up for you?

Expansion is not without its problems. A growth factor of 8.5 for the ten years between 1985 and 1995 has led to a massive influx of staff and a growth in the number of nationalities employed. The next stage in training is likely to involve cultural awareness. Whatever the physical resources on the aircraft, understanding and sensitivity to the needs of both customers and colleagues can make or break the experience. Emirates are well aware of the critical need for continuous training in this area; they are not alone. As we shall see in the next section, British Airways have a strong cultural awareness programme supporting their global network.

BRITISH AIRWAYS

According to their advertising, British Airways are the 'World's Favourite Airline'. At a time when most of the large global carriers were losing money, BA was making healthy profits. Compared with Emirates, BA are a giant amongst airlines. Whilst not the biggest in terms of aircraft, they carry more passengers to more destinations than most airlines. To do this with a consistently high service requires very careful selection and training of staff. In 1991 BA had no fewer than 228 aircraft with a further 68 on order. Fleet numbers fluctuate as older aircraft are sold, but these numbers put BA well up within the major airlines. They are one of the launch customers for the Boeing 777, and through a series of marketing agreements and partnerships, the BA livery is now seen on aircraft as widely different as Concorde and commuter DHC8s operating out of Plymouth, UK.

Formed in 1972 from the merger of British European Airways (BEA) and the British Overseas Airways Corporation (BOAC), BA was privatized by the Thatcher government in 1987. One of the new company's first actions was to acquire British Caledonian, also in that year. Latterly Caledonian, as it was rebranded, has operated the charter arm of BA, previously branded under the British Airtours label, but it was announced in December 1994 that Caledonian would be sold to a holiday company in the spring of 1995.

Since privatization, growth has occurred through direct expansion, through acquiring both minority and majority shareholdings in airlines such as US Air, Quantas, Brymon European, TAT (France); by setting up subsidiary operations, such as Deutsche BA and British Asia Airways; and by marketing agreements, for example with Maersk Air (Denmark) and Manx Airlines.

Such growth presents major problems of culture and consistency. When a partner's aircraft are painted in BA livery and/

or the check-in desks are manned by people who may work for the partner but are in BA uniforms, then the customer quite rightly expects a consistent BA standard of service. Given the huge route network – ranging from London to Japan, through to Birmingham to Aberdeen – this means that all staff need a common understanding of the values and standards of the airline. Like all organizations, BA doesn't 'get it right' all of the time, but given the size of the enterprise one should, perhaps, be surprised at how often they do provide a consistently high standard of service to a huge number of passengers. Whereas Emirates carried 200,000+ passengers in 1994, according to Leo Marriot (*British Airways*, 1993), in 1992 BA (including Caledonian) carried no fewer than 24,522,000, supported by a worldwide staff of over 50,000. Excluding destinations served by their partners, in 1993, BA had scheduled flights to nearly 200 destinations worldwide.

In order to meet the excellence criteria laid down earlier in this chapter, BA has an intensive training programme that goes far beyond the technical and safety aspects of the operation.

More than 300 staff a year, drawn from worldwide stations, undertake a Certificate in Management Studies programme (known as the 'Fundamentals of Supervision'; FOS). This open-learning programme has been supported by workshops/seminars in London, Gatwick, Manchester, Birmingham, Glasgow, New-castle, New Delhi and New York, to which participants fly in from their stations to attend. This programme can lead to a postgraduate Diploma in Business Administration (DBA), and thence to a Masters in Business Administration (MBA). There is a dedicated open-learning 'Fundamentals of Customer Service' (FOCS) programme, and during 1993 and 1994 the highly acclaimed 'Winning for Customers' and 'Managing Winners' programmes.

Winning for Customers was a one-day event for *all* of the airline's staff wherever they were based in the world. The programme used specially arranged facilities at London Heathrow and focused on how staff could assist and, in the case of problems, recover a customer. To fly in overseas staff and regional staff, arrange transport and accommodation and provide time off for both travel and the programme was a massive undertaking, but one BA judged worthwhile. As their Group Managing Director, Robert Ayling, pointed out: 'it costs five times as much to win a new customer as to retain an existing one.' Therefore, when things go wrong, the staff need to be able to use personal initiative to recover the situation; personal competence coming to the fore again. 'Managing Winners' was a programme for managers who needed to look at the skills they required to manage an empowered work-force.

Both Emirates and BA show a long-term commitment to excellence and the skills and competence of their staff; it is no coincidence that these are linked. Both airlines are re-equiping and expanding. Both use the latest technologies for passenger comfort: BA are currently (1995) undertaking trials with seat-mounted telephones for passenger use. Both airlines provide value for money and competitive fares, but neither compromise standards in an effort to woo customers by price alone. Both depend on the personal competence of their staff, especially those at the customer interface, for their continuing success.

THINK POINT

BA is a very large organization. How difficult do you believe it is for very large organizations to respond to customer needs, especially in a global environment? Have you experienced problems in receiving a flexible response from larger organizations?

PRINCESS CRUISES

(All shipping information is taken from *Great Passenger Ships of the World* by Arnold Klundas; *The 1994 Berlitz Complete Guide to Cruising and Cruise Ships* by Douglas Ward, and Princess Cruises' *Information to Passengers*.)

Much of the information in these notes relates to the MV (motor vessel) *Pacific Princess*, a 20,636-ton passenger vessel launched in Emden, West Germany, on 9 May 1970. Originally Norwegian owned and named the *Sea Venture*, she was sold to the P&O (Peninsular & Orient) to form part of their Los Angeles based Princess Cruise fleet in 1975. She was renamed *Pacific Princess*.

Readers may well remember the popular television series 'The Love Boat'; *Pacific Princess* was the original star of the show. Her sister ship, the *Island Princess* (originally the *Island Venture*) has a similar history.

Both ships are currently (1995) registered under the ownership of Abbey National March Leasing Ltd, chartered by P&O Lines Ship Owners of London, and operated by Princess Cruises of Los Angeles. Both vessels are registered in the UK, and fly the red ensign to denote the country of registration, the P&O houseflag and the Princess Cruise houseflag.

All Princess Cruises vessels carry the suffix 'Princess'.

In 1988 P&O acquired Sitmar Cruises, which led to a large expansion of the fleet. All the Sitmar vessels were renamed with the 'Princess' suffix and new names allocated to those vessels currently being built for Sitmar.

P&O are perhaps better known in the UK for their cruises based on the *Canberra* and the *Sea Princess*. A new vessel, the *Oriana*, entered service in 1995. They also operate an intensive cross-Channel service from ports such as Dover and Portsmouth. They are one of the UK's oldest shipping companies. Peninsular and Orient Steam Navigation, and Orient Lines, merged to form P&O in 1960, and were amongst the earliest shipping companies offering cruises – indeed, as early as the 1880s.

Providing consistency over such a wide range of operations is no easy task, but P&O are highly regarded worldwide for their quality of product.

The Princess fleet in 1995 comprised vessels that range in size from approximately 20,000 tons (*Pacific / Island /* and *Fair Princesses*, to be disposed of in 1995), up to 70,000 tons (*Crown* and *Regal Princesses*). New vessels on order are to be over 100,000 tons. In 1994 the Princess fleet comprised nine vessels.

Major cruising areas are the US west coast to Alaska, where Princess own hotel and railroad facilities; the Caribbean; US west coast–Panama Canal–Caribbean; Mediterranean; and Scandinavia. The two smallest ships, *Pacific* and *Island Princess*, work their ways round the world offering a variety of cruising opportunities. As will be illustrated later in this case study, different markets and areas require different vessels.

The *Berlitz Complete Guide* by Douglas Ward is published at regular intervals (most recently in 1994), and provides a wealth of information from which a choice of cruise can be made. Their ratings are used in the comparisons later in this case study.

Cruising is not cheap and therefore value for money is very important. Perhaps the first question to be asked is why people go on a cruise, what is it they are seeking? If the answer is connected with service, then the personal competence of the crew will be a very important factor in customer choice.

Cruising is generally very relaxing. Most ships provide entertainment, but it is optional. The food is normally very good, and international rather than local in character. Once on board you can go from place to place without having to unpack, since your hotel moves with you. Most ships provide medical facilities and most cruises go to where the sunshine is. Itineraries range from the exotic (like the Amazon), the adventurous (like the Antarctic), the spectacular (Alaska and Norway), the tropical (Caribbean and South Seas) and the historical (much of the Mediterranean).

The disadvantages are that you are never in a place very long, so you either have to book shore tours or not see very much. Seas can be 'lumpy' at times. As mentioned previously, cruises are not cheap, and accommodation, being on a ship, may be less luxurious than in many hotels, although many staterooms/cabins at sea have private *en suite* facilities (all Princess ships are so equipped), and standards are rising.

According to the Berlitz guide, in 1992 5,410,000 people cruised, of which 4,250,00 were from the USA, with UK citizens making up the next largest group with 225,000. These numbers are growing, and a number of new vessels are being commissioned.

Discussions with regular cruise passengers suggest that there are certain intangibles that make this form of holiday special. A study of excellence should seek to explore the roots of those intangibles.

The excellent cruise companies provide their customers with the illusion of their own personal vessel, with enough quiet places to be alone with that illusion, and standards of service that are both high and personal.

Ships such as the *Pacific Princess* are just so many thousand tons of steel, so the ship cannot be the deciding factor; the organization is headquartered thousands of miles away, and customers will rarely meet corporate staff, so the most important factor in achieving excellence and the personal illusion (as Tom Peters has said on many occasions) must be the people. The key to excellence must lie within the 354 crew members.

In the introduction to this volume, a model, first used in the first three volumes of *In Charge*, was introduced showing the link between tasks and the effectiveness and goals of the organization.

For a cruise to have been effective, all three competences – *personal, functional* and *organizational* – need to have been demonstrated and be in balance.

Before analsying the Princess operation in terms of the model, it is necessary to define what the desirable outcomes are.

For the passenger the prime concern is likely to be an overall enjoyable holiday experience. This can be split down into a number of sub-areas: an interesting itinerary to meet his or her needs, high-quality food, comfortable surroundings and accommodation, good entertainment, a mix of activities and convivial travelling companions. For the company, they will wish for supplementary income from duty-free sales, bar sales, shore excursions, etc., plus, most importantly, repeat customers who will return home and tell their relatives, friends and colleagues about their experience, and thus assist in generating new business.

Of the 634 passengers on a particular voyage, over 400 were members of 'The Captain's Circle', the Princess club for past passengers – a repeat business rate of 60 per cent. On the excellent 'Winning for Customers' course (see earlier) provided for all staff worldwide by British Airways, the point is made that it costs at least five times as much to gain a new customer as to keep an existing one, so high repeat business figures are a sound indication of organizational effectiveness.

THINK POINT

How important is repeat business to your organization? What percentage of your business comes from your existing customer base? Could this figure be improved, and how?

Whilst there is a complex organization chart for a vessel such as the *Pacific Princess* (indeed the ship could be regarded as an organization in its own right), from the passenger's point of view there are four main areas of operation, with the Captain in overall control and accountable for the first three. These equate to the various aspects of the Maslow model of motivation introduced in chapter 5 of *In Charge, Managing People*, and chapter 4 of this volume.

Transportation/safety aspects connected with the ship

Under the direct control of the Captain, the navigation, engineering, electrical (etc.) staff ensure that the voyage is completed on schedule, in safety and with as little inconvenience to the passengers as possible. Here the organization needs to meet the physiological and safety needs of the customers.

Hotel aspects

The 634 passengers need to be accommodated and fed. One can never complain about the quantity of food offered on a cruise: eating can start at 0600 and finish with the midnight buffet, with any number of meals and snacks in between. Laundry facilities need to be provided, staterooms kept clean and made up. Passengers need to acquire foreign currency, they may need medical attention, their accounts need to be kept up to date. Under the accountability of the Captain this role falls to the purser's department, a very large department indeed, helping to meet the physiological needs of the passengers.

Entertainment

Cruise ships provide a full range of entertainments and activities ranging from quizzes, deck games and cabaret to full-scale shows. There are shore excursions to be arranged, shops to be run and photographic services to be provided. Modern cruise ships have a full entertainments team, again under the ultimate control of the

Captain, but organized through the Cruise Director. The Cruise Director is the member of staff that the passengers will come to know most closely. Belonging, esteem and self-actualization needs in Maslow terms are the role of the Cruise Director and his or her staff.

Pre and post cruise

Passengers have to travel from home to their ship and return home again after the cruise. The vast majority of passengers will be making an air journey. So will their luggage, and so indeed may crew who are joining or leaving the ship.

The ship's passenger and crew lists for one particular voyage revealed the number of nationalities represented amongst the passengers and crew.

No less than 24 (12 of passengers and 24 of crew) nationalities were represented aboard the ship, all with their own cultural norms and needs.

Travel to and from the ship was arranged by Princess Cruises but was not under their direct control. When a passenger who has, in one case, travelled from Birmingham (Alabama) to Atlanta, Georgia, to London and then on to Venice on three different airlines, finds that their luggage has not arrived at the same time as they have, and goes to the purser's office, the company cannot and to their credit do not say that this is not their problem. Every effort is made to track down the luggage prior to sailing, and if it is not found immediately, toiletries and clothing vouchers are provided. There is always a problem for any organization that has to rely on third parties meeting their needs. An excellent organization will take ownership of these issues on behalf of the customer.

All of the organizations involved in getting the traveller to and from the ship, and responsible for his or her comfort when ashore, for airlines, hotels, excursion companies, etc., need to get it right first time if the experience is to be both enjoyable and memorable – and not memorable for the wrong reason. In the case of third-party activities booked by the company, they are likely to receive the blame if things go wrong even if they are beyond their control.

There can be tensions between the four areas. The ship may have to sail before a missing item of luggage is recovered. Indeed, passengers on shore excursions may, through their own fault, miss the ship and need to be recovered. Essential maintenance may require that some facilities are temporarily unavailable. Sailing times and meal times may conflict. The organization needs to function in a holistic manner. Most passengers never realize the depth and complexity of planning that occurs. On a trip through the Bosporous everything had been planned to ensure the ship was at the entrance to the Dardanelles for a certain time to fit in with shipboard activities and the timed arrival in Athens the next morning. The fact that there were a considerable number of small boats in a narrower channel and a slow moving freighter ahead of *Pacific Princess* as she wound her way through a difficult waterway, probably went unnoticed by the vast majority of passengers who gained an exciting, second view of the splendours of Istanbul, but provided the navigators with a test of their skills.

All staff need to be *functionally competent*. The Captain needs to be a competent seaman, the chefs need to be able to cook properly, the singers need good voices, the shore excursion staff need to know about the ports of call.

The organization needs *organisational competence*. It needs to be committed to its customers, it needs systems and procedures in place to deal with foreign immigration and customs procedures; it needs effective staff rotas and training programmes. The entertainments and activities need to reflect the cultural mix of passengers so that nobody feels left out. If this means changing the line in 'There'll always be an England', featured in one of the shows, from 'The Empire too, we can depend on you' to 'America too. . .', then so be it: artistic licence to meet cultural needs is perfectly acceptable except to the purist.

Part of the organizational competence that goes a long way to creating the personal illusion is that the *Pacific Princess* carries fewer passengers than many other similar sized vessels. The Berlitz guide shows that her maximum complement, every berth filled, is 717. This can be compared with three similar sized competitors that can carry a maximum of 959, 898 and 925 passengers respectively. Given that most staterooms only contain two people, the figures based on two-berth capacity are 610 for the *Pacific Princess* and 804, 704, and 700 respectively for her competitors. This gives a much higher passenger to space ratio, and the figures for crew to passengers reflect this decision to avoid any overcrowding.

There is a potential downside for the passenger. Less passengers means slightly higher prices, but as the model for the first two of the 4 Ps of marketing, *product, price, promotion* and *place* (covered in chapter 1 of *In Charge, Managing Operations*) suggests, customers' decisions are made by selecting the product they require at the price they are prepared to pay. An analysis of passengers on voyage 4419 shows that they were mainly 40+ years old, there were few children, and passengers were prepared to pay extra for more space. Other ships in the company cater for a different market, although the Berlitz ratings for Princess suggest that the company is not filling every nook and cranny with cabins and that there has been a conscious decision to go for space and to charge slightly more.

Whilst functional and organizational competence should be assumed as being present, personal competence is a different matter. At this stage it is necessary to give a few personal examples of the level of service provided.

The Maître d'Hôtel and the bar waiters after two days seemed to know everybody's names. The relief cabin steward, on having a faulty shower reported to him, took ownership of the problem and took the offending fitting away to have it repaired rather than sending for an engineer. Given that the regular stewardess was off duty this was an unexpected example of personal competence. A meal that was properly prepared and cooked but not liked, was changed without question. Junior staff showed a genuine concern that people were enjoying themselves, staff who one would not be tipping directly. Senior officers and staff, especially the Captain, were visible around the ship talking to passengers on a casual, informal basis, and not just at formal cocktail parties.

These are just a few examples of personal competence. There is no doubt that such personal competence can only work in a situation where functional and organizational competence are demonstrated. Indeed, they would be futile without the other two competences. The model cannot stand without all three being present.

Senior staff in Princess are home grown, an idea that both Emirates and BA encourage; they have been with the company for a long time and understand its culture and mission. Junior staff come from diverse backgrounds: a wine steward with a BA (Hons.) in hotel management, gaining experience for a few years, a shop assistant waiting to join the Royal navy, a Mexican waiter sending money home – how do they achieve the necessary personal competence?

The driving force must come from the top, from the standards set throughout the fleet by the corporate headquarters in Los Angeles, from the P&O traditions, and most important, when one considers that there are nine ships separated by thousands of miles, by the example set by the Captain and senior officers.

All new staff follow the induction model proposed in chapter 7 of *In Charge, Managing People*.

1 There is a safety induction, for passengers will assume that any crew member is fully conversant with all safety aspects, perhaps not realizing that the crew member may have just joined their new ship;
2 there is a task induction, where crew members are trained in what may be very new tasks;
3 and there is an induction that deals with the personal competences, what the company stands for, pride in the ship, meeting the needs of customers.

Not everything goes well all the time, witness the non-functioning shower. What is impressive is the way situations are recovered, and when there are problems beyond the company's control, such as delays in landing due to local formalities, etc., passengers are kept informed. Customer recovery when there is a problem is a key factor in personal competence and excellence. Princess Cruises staff seem well versed in such actions.

Pacific Princess is just one vessel out of nine. On the Berlitz rating of 1, 1+ to 5+ stars, together with scores out of 2000, *Pacific Princess* and her sister ship *Island Princess* score 4+ stars. The lowest Princess score is 3 stars (this vessel was due for replacement in 1995), and the highest (*Royal Princess*) has 5 stars and a rating of 1751. The Princess ratings have a range of 1531 to 1751, and the average score is 1692, with only two scores out of the nine falling below the average. This highlights the statistical difficulty with using averages, mentioned in chapter 9 of *In Charge,*

Managing Finance and Information. These scores, given that Princess Cruises are by no means the dearest on the market, show considerable consistency.

All organizations that operate on a wide geographical basis have problems with consistency of product. Given that different operating areas meet the needs of different markets with different age groups and passenger requirements an objective rating scheme is very hard to devise. A ship can score highly on entertainment factors that would not be appreciated by the passenger wishing for a quiet cruise, for example. The rating scheme of Douglas Ward for the Berlitz guide, combining as it does objective ratings with subjective comments, should be of considerable use for anybody planning a cruise.

That personal competences are important is shown by the entries for two sister ships (not the *Pacific Princess* and *Island Princess*), both owned by Princess Cruises. Both have 4+ stars, one scores 1743 points and the other 1732. Whilst these are both very high scores, given that Berlitz ratings in 1994 ranged from 1830–131 over 189 ships, and these ships were numbers 32 and 41 (eight out of the nine Princess ships are in the top 50 per cent), all of the differences in individual rating areas in the guide are connected with personal competence. The ships score identically for appearance, comfort, etc.

Princess Cruises offer an excellent product, what inconsistencies there are across the fleet can be explained by age and markets. There will always be a place for the smaller ship: they can go up the Amazon, 100,000 ton vessels cannot. Slightly older ships acquire characters of their own, but at the end of the day, the experience will depend on the personal competences of the staff at the front end, the stewards and stewardesses, waiters, pool attendants, hairdressers, and others. They have the most contact with customers and it is they who can put things right in the first instance. The Captain of the *Pacific Princess* in 1994, Captain David Christie, in conversation was only too clear that it is these staff who make or break a company. They need and have adequate accommodation, they appear to be valued by the company and they make the passenger experience not just good but excellent.

Princess are not alone in offering an excellent product, just as Emirates and BA are not the only excellent airlines. Having read this volume of *In Charge*, you need to consider what you regard as excellence and the personal competences you need to demonstrate so that your customers will look at your products and service in terms of excellence and customer commitment.

All three organizations depend upon others for the totality of their product. BA invited prime suppliers to take part in 'Winning for Customers', because they don't own airports, and their flights may be handled by third parties. Princesss don't own the airlines that fly passengers to their ships, and so on. These companies keep as careful eye on the third-party ball as they do on their own, and all three are very much aware that it is the people in the third-party organizations and not necessarily the organizations themselves that can make or break the product. Personal competence is the biggest aid to customer recovery: organizations like those above have recognized this and encouraged the development of personal competence skills.

THINK POINT

Are there any similarities between the approaches to customer service taken by Emirates, BA or Princess that are reflected in the way you operate at work? How can you assist your organization in achieving excellence?

10
Action Plan

ACTION PLAN 1: BACK ANALYSIS

a) Baggage

What events in the past have most influenced where you are, what you do, and who you're with now? List the most important.

Write a brief description of your current comfort zone under the following headings:

HOME

JOB

FAMILY

MONEY

b) Aspirations

Being realistic, what do you want to be doing:

One year from now?

Five years from now?

Ten years from now?

Are there any aspirations others have for you? List them, plus your feelings about them.

c)   *Culture*

Culture can be defined in terms of *values, attitudes* and *beliefs.* In a few sentences for each, try to analyse these in terms of your personal:

VALUES

ATTITUDES

BELIEFS

d) Knowledge

List below, first, any special qualifications you may hold; then skills you believe that you can demonstrate competence of; and finally, any special aptitudes you believe you have.

QUALIFICATIONS

SKILLS

APTITUDES

ACTION PLAN 2: TEAM ROLES

Write down the three team roles that you believe most apply to you:

ACTION PLAN 3:   PEST ANALYSIS

POLITICAL

ECONOMIC

SOCIAL

TECHNOLOGICAL

ACTION PLAN 4: SWOT ANALYSIS

STRENGTHS

WEAKNESSES

OPPORTUNITIES

THREATS

You should now have a fairly comprehensive picture of where you are.

ACTION PLAN 5: MANAGING CHANGE

Perform a Force Field Analysis on a recent, a current or an anticipated change, identifying drivers and restrainers. Indicate how restrainers were, are being or will be reduced to allow for the change to proceed.

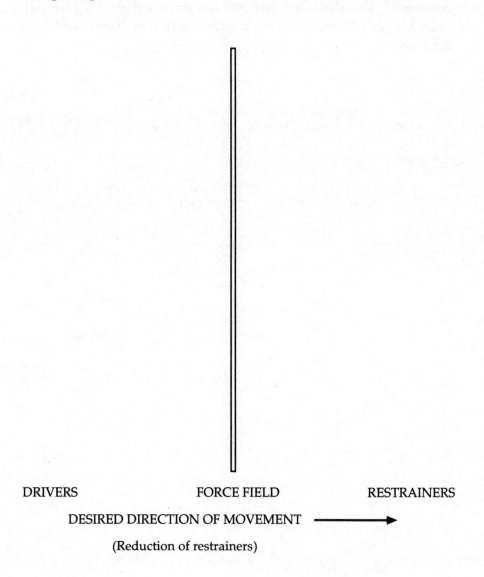

DRIVERS   FORCE FIELD   RESTRAINERS

DESIRED DIRECTION OF MOVEMENT ⟶

(Reduction of restrainers)

ACTION PLAN 6: POSITIVE THINKING

Make a list of things you want to achieve within the next year. They can be work goals, material goals, family goals, etc.

Write them down using the ideas above, 'I enjoy ...', etc. Remember they have already happened as far as your brain is concerned. Visualize each one at least once a day.

In a year's time, look back. How many of them have you achieved?

ACTION PLAN 7: PLANNING

Take an activity you need to plan for and use the Ten Step Planning Model introduced above to develop a preferred alternative for implementation.

After the task is completed, consider whether the plan worked using the ideas in the section.

DECIDE ON OBJECTIVES   *write them down*

ARE THE OBJECTIVES IN
LINE WITH PERSONAL AND   *if no, you will need to*
WORK CONSTRAINTS?   *amend the objectives*

WHAT ALTERNATIVES WILL
HELP TO ACHIEVE THE
OBJECTIVES?   *list them*

ASSESS THE CONSEQUENCES   *if the consequences present*
FOR EACH ALTERNATIVE   *major problems, discard or*
                                 file

ASSESS THE RESOURCES
NEEDED FOR EACH
ALTERNATIVE REMAINING

list them

CHOOSE THE ALTERNATIVE
WITH THE LEAST
PROBLEMATIC
CONSEQUENCES AND THE
LEAST RESOURCE
IMPLICATIONS AS YOUR
MAJOR STRATEGY

record it

USE OTHER REMAINING
ALTERNATIVES AS
CONTINGENCIES

list them

GATHER RESOURCES

record them as they are in place

AS THIS TAKES TIME, CHECK
BACK TO SEE THAT YOUR
OBJECTIVES HAVE NOT
CHANGED

MOVE TO IMPLEMENTATION
PHASE

At the end of the task ask yourself:

DID I DO WHAT I WANTED TO DO?

DID THE PLAN WORK?

WHAT CHANGES WERE MADE TO THE PLAN:
1) during planning:

2) during implementation as a result of monitoring.

HOW WOULD I DO IT DIFFERENTLY NEXT TIME?

ACTION PLAN 8: EXCELLENCE

Think back over the past few weeks. How have you demonstrated excellence? Give examples. On the other side of the sheet
detail improvements you could have made.

EVIDENCE   *IMPROVEMENTS*

a. SERVICE

b. CONSISTENCY

c. QUALITY

d. VALUE FOR MONEY

ACTION PLAN 9

Identify a project at work that you would like to be involved in

Now identify who can help you to become involved

ACTION PLAN 10

Think of two new ideas that you could try out in your organization

Idea 1:

Idea 2:

ACTION PLAN 11: ADOPT A CAN DO APPROACH

List your two tasks and identify how you will adopt a Can Do approach using the following headings:

Task 1 ....

    Thought ....

    Actions ....

    Manner of communicating ....

    Body language ....

Task 2 ....

    Thought ....

    Actions ....

    Manner of communicating ....

    Body language ....

ACTION PLAN 12: STRESS

Do you ever suffer from stress?

Can you recognize the symptoms? WHAT ARE THEY?

List some coping strategies

Identify the real cause

List your options:

Select preferred option

What changes will you make?

ACTION PLAN 13

TIME DIARY

DAY.................... DATE..................... PAGE No....................

Activity   *Start*   *End*   *Duration*   *Comments*

ACTION PLAN 14

List aspects of your life that might cause resentment

Have they been discussed? If not, why not?

What steps have been taken to resolve them?

ACTION PLAN 15

jobs you can delegate	to whom	training needed	benefits

ACTION PLAN 16

List examples of tasks given, by whom?

What action can you take

ACTION PLAN 17:   FRONT ANALYSIS

FORWARD

REVIEW

OPEN

NEW PLANS

TAKE OPPORTUNITIES

Appendix: MCI Personal Competence Model

The MCI suggest that for supervisors and managers to perform effectively they should consider the following personal competences.

Examine each in turn to see how you rate yourself.

Personal Competence		Units
Acting assertively	• take a leading role in initiating action and taking decisions	C12 D1
	• take personal responsibility for making things happen	C1 C4 C12
	• take control of situations and events	C12
	• act in an assured and unhesitating manner when faced with a challenge	C15 D1
	• say no to unreasonable requests	C1 C4 D1
	• state your own position and views clearly in conflict situations	C7 C9 C15
	• maintain your beliefs, commitment and effort in spite of set-backs or opposition	C7 C9 C15
Behaving ethically	• comply with legislation, industry regulation, professional and	C7 C15

organizational codes

	• show integrity and fairness in decision making	C7 C15
Building teams	• actively build relationships with others	C4 C12 D1
	• make time available to support others	C4 C9 C12 C15
	• encourage and stimulate others to make the best use of their abilities	C9 C12 C15
	• evaluate and enhance people's capability to do their jobs	C9 C12
	• provide feedback designed to improve people's future performance	C4 C9 C12
	• show respect for the views and actions of others	C4 C12 C15 D1
	• show sensitivity to the needs and feelings of others	C4 C12 C15 D1
	• use power and authority in a fair and equitable manner	C9 C12 C15
	• keep others informed about plans and progress	C4 C9 C12 A1
	• clearly identify what is required of others	C12 C15 A1
	• invite others to contribute to planning and organizing work	C9 C12 A1 D1
	• set objectives that are both achievable and challenging	C9 C12
	• use a variety of techniques to promote morale and productivity	C12 C15
	• check individuals' commitment to a specific course of action	C12 C15
	• identify and resolve causes of conflict or resistance	C12 C15
Communicating	• identify the information needs of listeners/audience	C1 C4 C9 A1 B1 D1

	• adopt/use communication styles appropriate to listeners and situations, including selecting an appropriate time and place	C4 C7 C9 C12 A1 B1 D1
	• use a variety of media and communication aids to reinforce points and maintain interest	C9 A1 D1
	• listen actively, ask questions, clarify points and rephrase others' statements to check mutual understanding	C4 C7 C9 C12 C15 B1 D1
	• encourage listeners to ask questions or rephrase statements to clarify their understanding	C1 C7 C9 C15 D1
	• modify communication in response to feedback from listeners	C1 C7 C9 C12 C15 D1
	• confirm listeners' understanding through questioning and inter-pretation of non-verbal signals	C7 C9 C12 D1
	• present difficult ideas and problems in a way that promotes understanding	C9
Focusing on results	• maintain a focus on objectives	C1 C15 A1 B1
	• tackle problems and take advantage of opportunities as they arrive	C1 A1 B1
	• monitor quality of work and progress against plans	C15 A1
	• Prioritize objectives and schedule work to make the best use of objectives	C1 B1
	• establish and communicate high expectations of performance, including setting an example to others	C15
	• actively seek to do things better	A1

	• use change as an opportunity for improvement	A1
	• continually strive to identify and minimize barriers to excellence	C15
Influencing others	• present yourself positively to others	C7 D1
	• use a variety of means to influence others	D1
	• create and prepare strategies for influencing others	C7
	• understand the culture of your organization and work within it or influence it	C7
Managing self	• take responsibility for meeting own learning and development needs	C1
	• seek feedback on performance to identify strengths and weaknesses	C1
	• learn from own mistakes and those of others	C1
	• change behaviour where needed as a result of feedback	C1
	• accept personal comments or criticism without becoming defensive	C4
	• remain calm in difficult or uncertain situations	C4
	• handle others' emotions without becoming personally involved in them	C4
Searching for information	• actively encourage the free exchange of information	C7
	• establish information networks to search for and gather relevant information	D1
	• make best use of existing sources of information	C7 D1
	• seek information from multiple sources	C7 D1

	• challenge the validity and reliability of sources of information	C7 D1
	• push for concrete information in an ambiguous situation	C7 D1
Thinking and decision taking	• break processes down into tasks and activities	C1 C7 C9 C12 A1
	• identify implications, consequences or causal relation-ships in a situation	C1 A1
	• take decisions which are realistic for the situation	C1 C4 C7 C9 C12 A1 B1 D1
	• produce a variety of solutions before taking a decision	C1 B1 D1
	• make use of, and reconcile a variety of perspectives when making sense of a situation	C4 B1 D1
	• identify a range of elements in and perspectives on a situation	A1
	• produce your own ideas from experience and practice	C4 B1 D1
	• focus on facts, problems and solutions when handling an emotional situation	C4
	• identify patterns or meaning from events and data that are not obviously related	C7
	• use your own experience and evidence from others to identify problems and understand situations	C9

The above is hard going, and yet we owe the authors and generators of the Personal Competence Model a great debt. They have produced a set of personal competences that you can take and adapt to your situation. The scenario that you have seen in this book is designed to show you how personal competences are put into practice.

References

Adams, J., Hayes, J. and Hopson B. (1976), *Transitions – Understanding and Managing Personal Change*. Oxford, Martin Robertson.

Barrett, J. and Williams, G. (1980), *Test Your Own Aptitude*. London, Kogan Page.

Belbin, M. (1981), *Management Teams, Why They Succeed or Fail*. London, Heinemann.

Buchanan, D. and Huczynski, H. (1985), *Organizational Behaviour*. London, Prentice Hall.

Hastings, C., Bixby, P. and Chaudry-Lawton, R. (1986), *Superteams – A Blueprint for Organisational Success*. London, Gower.

Holmes, T. H. and Rahe, R. J. (1967), 'The Social Readjustment Rates Scale', *Journal of Psychosomatic Research*, 11, 213–18.

Honey, P. and Mumford, A. (1990), *A Manual of Learning Styles*. Maidenhead, P. Honey.

Klundas, A. (1992), *Great Passenger Ships of the World Today*. Sparkford, Patrick Stephens.

Kolb, D. (1979), *Organizational Psychology: An Experiential Approach*. New Jersey, Prentice Hall.

Laborde, G. (1988), *Fine Tune Your Brain*. Palo Alto, Syntony Publishing.

Lewin, K. (1951), *Field Theory in Social Science*, ed. Dowin-Cartwright. New York, Harper.

Likert, R. (1961), *New Patterns of Management*. New York, McGraw-Hill.

Luft, J. and Ingham, H. (1955), *The Johari Window – A Graphic Model of Interpersonal Awareness*, in the Proceedings of the Western Training Laboratory in Group Development, Los Angeles, UCLA.

McGregor, D. (1960), *The Human Side of Enterprise*. New York, McGraw-Hill.

Margerison, C. J. and McCann, D. J. (1985), *How to Lead a Winning Team*. Bradford, University of Bradford Press.

Marriot, L. (1993), *British Airways*. Shepperton, Ian Allan.

Peters, T. (1987), *Thriving on Chaos*. New York, Alfred A. Knopf Inc.

Peters, T. and Waterman, R. (1981), *In Search of Excellence*. New York, Harper & Row.

Tice, L. (1989), *Investment in Excellence* (multi media). Seattle, Pacific Institute.

Trompenaars, F. (1993), *Riding the Waves of Culture*. London, Economist Books.

Ward, D. (1994), *The Berlitz Complete Guide to Cruising and Cruise Ships 1994*. Oxford, Berlitz.

Index